TOUCHING
THE FATHER'S
HEART

CESAR CASTELLANOS D

Cesar Castellanos © 2005
Published by G12 Editores
sales@g12bookstore.com

ISBN 1-932285-64-4

www.visiong12.com
www.g12bookstore.com

Printed in USA

| editors |

CONTENTS

INTRODUCTION

As you read through the pages of this book, you will discover a God that is a real spiritual being who is aware of each and every one of His beloved children's needs. Your faith will increase as you know and acknowledge that your future depends solely on Him. God will be as big as you believe Him to be. In other words, God's greatness in your life depends on the type of faith you possess.

How can we touch our Heavenly Father's heart? The only way is through His Son, Jesus Christ. "The Father loves the Son, and has given all things into His hand. He who believes in the Son has everlasting life; and he who does not believe the Son shall not see life, but the wrath of God abides on him" (John 3:35-36).

The key to touching the Father's heart depends on how we relate to Him. Thus, the importance of understanding, knowing, and practicing each step is found in the precious prayer that Jesus taught, will enable you to live a supernatural experience on a daily basis.

In this simple prayer, you will discover the keys that unlock the Kingdom of Heaven. "So I say to you, ask, and it will be given to you; seek, and you will find; knock, and it will be opened to you. For everyone who asks receives and he who seeks finds, and to him who knocks it will be opened" (Luke 11:9-10).

The Psalmist expressed: "The LORD is near to all who call upon Him, to all who call upon Him in truth" (Psalm 145:18). He is closer than the air we breathe. Sadly, many have fallen into religiosity because they do not know how to relate to God. He longs to have personal contact with us through prayer. The Holy Bible contains more than thirty-two thousand promises of blessings which can only be understood and claimed through prayer.

God has given each one of us a measure of faith. This is the key that we possess to conquer what seems impossible in the natural. Paul said: "...as God has dealt to each one a measure of faith" (Romans 12:3).

You may think you have no faith, but I want you to know that you have faith within you. You must begin to develop it through your prayer life. The Lord Jesus said: "...assuredly, I say to you, if you have faith as a mustard seed, you will say to this mountain, 'Move from here to there,' and it will move; and nothing will be impossible for you" (Matthew 17:20).

The mustard seed is the smallest seed of all. Its size can be compared to that of a sowing pin's head. The Lord chose this example to teach us that He chooses the tiniest thing to conquer the greatest, and all things that seem impossible.

Faith comes as a result of spending time daily in God's presence. It is in that secret place of intimacy with God that we receive revelation of scripture, faith, and direction for our lives. This gives us the ability to meet our desired goals, as long as our prayers are specific.

God longs to touch our hearts. Many times He will permit adverse circumstances in our lives so that we can listen to His voice. A couple of years after Claudia and I got married, we experienced a severe financial crisis. Our daughter Johanna was young, and our finances were slowly dwindling away. Although I worked hard, I was unable to see a way out from this crisis. One evening, I arrived home so overwhelmed and afflicted that I began to weep. My intention was to complain to God, but He did not allow it. Before I started praying, God's anointing fell upon me and I started speaking in other tongues, which released a supernatural strength and power that left me in awe.

The Lord immediately gave me the interpretation. He said to me: "Most assuredly I say unto you, I will bless you to such a degree that you will be in shock and will tell me, 'That is enough, that's too much!'"

I marveled when I heard those words, because that had never even crossed my mind. When I stood up from being on my face before God, I felt like the most prosperous man in the world. I ran to tell my wife what had occurred, and together we believed God's Word and saw a major blessing in our finances.

The book of Hebrews teaches us that faith is the substance of things hoped for. It is vital that we understand that the word "substance" is derived from a Greek word that means: "Legal title deed to a property." When you believe God, you become pregnant with faith in Him that moves you into a supernatural realm, and with your title deed you can claim the blessings that God has in store for you. Every time that I have longed to see great miracles, I was required to take a step of faith and believe that I had a legal title deed to a property. This is an argument in my favor which I present before God, then I confront the enemy with faith and tell him: "I claim my legal rights and command you to let go of my finances, family, blessings and church."

You must renew your mind to the point that you have the conviction that the Father has given you substance. With this, you will be able to see every circumstance, not with your natural eyes, but through God's eyes. You will begin to think, talk, and dream like He does. Having done that, you will no longer be a person of failure, but will begin to be a successful and prosperous person. Your home will not be in ruins, but you will live in harmony. You will not see your church weak, but you will see it as a prosperous church that is experiencing unprecedented growth. The miracle must first occur in your mind. Allow the Lord to renew your mind through the lessons found in this book, because the Lord desires for you to enter into a new dimension of intimacy with Him.

Preparing Ourselves to Relate to God

"I don't know how to pray!" I can't last ten minutes without having all sorts of thoughts go through my mind!" This is a common condition I have found in thousands of people I have met.

The power to communicate with our Creator in prayer, is one of the greatest privileges that we have been given.

This is the means by which God allows us to relate directly with Him. Jesus did not teach His disciples how to preach; however, He did teach them how to pray.

In the early days of my Christian life, I found myself praying in my bedroom one day. I was praying with fear because I imagined a God that was sitting on His throne with a whip in hand ready to punish anyone who disobeyed Him. While I was praying with that attitude, I heard a still small voice speak to the deepest part of my heart, saying: "Who told you that God is like that? Don't you know that His arms are opened wide waiting to embrace you?"

In an act of faith, I immediately ran into those arms which were opened wide for me. Ever since that day, I have related to God as my one true Father. Although I lost my earthly father when I was ten years old, I can honestly say that after having this personal experience with the Lord in my bedroom, all the emptiness that once existed in me was filled with His presence.

The author of Hebrews said: "Let us draw near with a true heart in full assurance of faith, having our hearts sprinkled from an evil conscience and our bodies washed with pure water" (Hebrews 10:22).

"Teach us to pray the way John taught his disciples," was what the disciples requested of the Lord. I believe that every believer should have the same disposition that these men had. Jesus proceeded to teach them the most important prayer of all ages: "The Lord's Prayer" (see Matthew 6:5-13).

He demonstrated the three essential steps that we must take in order for our prayers to be effective. Although our Lord Jesus taught us that we can pray at all times and in any place, He requires a certain attitude in our hearts so that we can effectively communicate with Him.

The Jews had turned prayer into an external act that was accompanied with gestures, movements, and repetitive words expressed in a mechanical form. This had caused the religious leaders of those days to fall into hypocrisy, giving greater importance to the external rather than to the internal attitude of the heart.

We must believe that His ear will be open to hear our prayers if we sincerely desire to speak to Him.

"Now this is the confidence that we have in Him, that if we ask anything according to His will, He hears us" (1 John 5:14).

First Step: Have a Sincere Heart

The Pharisees boasted, claiming to be super spiritual. For this reason, Jesus placed the mark of "hypocrites" upon their foreheads. Although they did many good things like pray, fast, and give offerings, they made the serious mistake of doing this to obtain the respect and admiration of others. They subtly concealed the sin that was in their hearts and had others believing that they were righteous, without caring about the fact that their relationship with God was in shambles.

Something similar occurred with King Saul when he did not care about the fact that God had rejected him, and cared more about his appearance before others and begged the prophet Samuel to guard his image before the people.

The first word of advice that the Lord gave to the disciples was to have a sincere heart. He warned them: "Therefore do not be like them. For your Father knows the things you have need of before you ask Him" (Matthew 6:8).

As we draw near to God, we must do so with total sincerity. Many try to cover their sins with excuses. They have never experienced freedom, because they have not confessed their sins. If you have sinned, do not justify it, confront it. Only when you sincerely repent will you be able to relate to God in prayer.

If you excuse your mistakes, you will never have the conviction to repent and your life will continue as it is.

The Psalmist David asked: "Who can understand his errors? Cleanse me from secret faults. Keep back Your servant also from presumptuous sins; let them not have dominion over me. Then I shall be blameless and I shall be innocent of great transgression" (Psalm 19:12-13). Then King Solomon said: "The hypocrite with his mouth destroys his neighbor…" (Proverbs 11:9a). "But the hypocrites in heart store up wrath; they do not cry for help when He binds them" (Job 36:13). The Lord Jesus said it this way: "And why do you look at the speck in your brother's eye, but do not consider the plank in your own eye? Or how can you say to your brother, 'Let me remove the speck from your eye'; and look, a plank is in your own eye? Hypocrite! First remove the plank from your own eye, and then you will see clearly to remove the speck from your brother's eye" (Matthew 7:3-5).

Hypocrites cannot see their own defects, but rather, they live constantly looking at other's mistakes.

The Lord exhorted the Scribes and Pharisees, telling them: "Hypocrites! Well did Isaiah prophesy about you, saying: 'These people draw near to Me with their mouth, and honor Me with their lips, but their heart is far from Me. And in vain they worship Me, teaching as doctrines the commandments of men'" (Matthew 15:7-9).

Second Step: Privacy

Prayer is a private conversation with God. That is why the Lord spoke about going into the secret place–a place where you can be intimate with Him in private. It is true that you can pray anywhere at anytime, but Matthew teaches of a moment of privacy with God (see Matthew 6:4). We must seek for the opportune time to be alone in His presence.

Some prefer it early in the morning, others in the afternoon, and others late in the evening. The most important thing is that you set aside a time to talk with God. Remember that our God is Spirit and He desires that we worship Him in spirit and in truth.

The prayer in secret is an experience that is similar to that of marital intimacy; this is where God relates to us and we enter into deep intimacy with His Spirit. Every believer needs a place where they can have a private time with God on a daily basis. It could be an office, a bedroom, a living room, or any other place. The Lord Jesus did not have a specific place, so He chose to pray outdoors in the early hours of the morning (see Mark 1:35).

The Psalmist Asaph had an internal battle as he witnessed how the wicked prospered. Because of this strong attack, he gave place to envy, and was able to understand the end that awaits the wicked as he entered the sanctuary. "Until I went into the sanctuary of God, then I understood their end. Surely You set them in slippery places; You cast them down to destruction" (Psalm 73:17-18).

We can learn so much about prayer in reading the psalms. David said: "He restores my soul…" (Psalm 23:3a). In spite of the fact that he was in great anguish, prayer became a true comfort to his soul–a spiritual renewing force that strengthened him so that he could keep moving forward. When Jesus told the disciples to lay their burdens on Him, He was inviting them through prayer to trust Him for their needs, knowing that He would supply whatever they needed and deliver them from doubt, fear and anxiety. God would give them the peace that surpasses all understanding.

The Lord said through the prophet Isaiah: "Come, my people, enter your chambers and shut your doors behind you; hide yourself, as it were, for a little moment, until the indignation is past" (Isaiah 26:20).

Third Step: Do Not Use Vain Repetition

Avoid constant repetition when you pray. Try not to appeal to mere words. Do not turn prayer into a series of repetitive words that make no sense. Many people take this prayer and repeat it excessively, believing that the more they repeat it, the more effective it will be. The Lord warned the disciples not to repeat the same prayer in cycles. The Ephesians were the ones who did this: "But when they found out that he was a Jew, all with one voice cried out for about two hours, 'Great is Diana of the Ephesians'" (Acts 19:34). Repetitive prayer was the norm in pagan circles, but not among God's people.

"Hear my prayer, O God; give ear to the words of my mouth" (Psalm 54:2). In his sincere prayer, the Psalmist reasoned with God the same way that a man would reason with his friend. I do not consider it punishment to speak with my wife, quite the contrary, I enjoy it. So it is with prayer. We must do it with joy, happiness and understanding; never as a requirement or an obligation.

The apostle James said: "You ask and do not receive, because you ask amiss, that you may spend it on your pleasures" (James 4:3). Although God requests that every one of His children pray daily, certain prayers go unanswered because they lack faith. Without faith it is impossible to please God. This is why mechanical prayers do not please Him—they lack faith.

Upon introducing these words, the Lord unlocked the doors for us to have permanent open communication with the Father. "The effectual prayer of the righteous avails much" (James 5:16b). As we understand, learn, and practice these ten levels of prayer, we will daily discover the most beneficial aspects of our daily life.

Chapter 1

KNOWING GOD AS OUR FATHER

"Our Father..." (Matthew 6:9)

The highest position a man could ever aspire to have in life is to be a father. God called Abram, whose name means "exalted father," to serve Him. God chose to enter into an eternal covenant relationship with him and all of his descendants. In order for the promise to be fulfilled, God had to change his name to Abraham, "the father of multitudes" (see Genesis 17:4-5).

The closest thing to God's heart is a father's heart. Sadly, the concept of fatherhood is quite distorted these days. Dr. Derek Prince once shared that someone had described a father as: "A father is an executive who always carries a briefcase and is never home." When he heard that, he cried out: "My God, I don't want to be that kind of father."

The cause behind rebellious youth, violence, family crisis, divorce and separation, are all the consequences of men who have not taken their rightful place of authority. Man has resigned his fatherhood to become a selfish person that only thinks about making money. Although he uses the excuse that he is working hard to provide for his children, in reality, he thrives on feeding his own ego.

JESUS GAVE US THE GOAL OF FATHERHOOD

In sharing the Sermon on the Mount, our Lord Jesus said: "Therefore you shall be perfect, just as your Father in heaven is perfect" (Matthew 5:48). Jesus set the standard for every disciple. He did not tell us to work hard and be savvy in business, although it is important. What He expressed speaks about the measure which He wants us to attain: to be a father who has the same compassionate heart that the Heavenly Father possesses. The crisis we are facing is in men who are suffering in the area of fatherhood, because men do not have a clear revelation of what the responsibility of having children truly is.

When Jesus taught us to pray, He revealed something great to us: the Father of all is God.

Delegated Authority

The apostle Paul stated: "…from whom the whole family in heaven and earth is named" (Ephesians 3:15). If you were to read the original declaration, it would say: "From whom the family of heaven and earth derives its name." When we are talking about family here, it is referring to paternity. God gave men the ability to be fathers; He entrusted His authority unto them. This delegated authority consists in that God, being Father of all, delegates His authority to human beings and trusts them with it.

God said: "I will not be a Father directly to you, rather, I will be a father through you." God uses the seed of man to fulfill His purpose. He could have been my daughters' father, but He entrusted that responsibility to me and gave me four precious women to care for. The most important thing for me to understand is that God entrusted them to me so that I may behave in the same manner in which He would: with responsibility, fondness, affection, expressing love and approval, providing for their needs (not only material, but the emotional needs as well), and above all, teaching them about the spiritual and faith in God. The day the Heavenly Father calls me home and demands that I be accountable for what I did on earth, the first thing that He will ask me is: "What did you do with the talent I gave you of fatherhood? How did you lead your family? What principles did you instill in them? Did they see Me in you?" God will examine me to see if I was a proper or improper father.

The moment I understood that God had given me His authority in order for me to represent Him as a father, I abandoned myself to do everything that the Heavenly Father would do for my daughters. I planted a garden of love. I love my girls dearly and I demonstrate it daily, because I am aware that love is what gives them security, stability and confidence, which motivates them to conquer and be successful. When a man is verbally or physically abusive to his wife, the children will perceive it, which causes them to be deeply hurt. Many times they may even come to hate their father, because of the abusive manner in which he treated their mother and siblings. So many children have grown up with a broken heart, full of resentment, which came as a result of the humiliation they went through with their parents. My daughters have never seen an embarrassing scene at home. They have never seen me abuse my wife, neither have they seen her abuse me with words, attitudes or actions. We have always strived to have a home that would bring joy to God's heart. We try to never hurt our daughters and never punish them unjustly because we have understood that many times if a child is disciplined incorrectly, a wall of separation is built between the father and the family.

Decide to Teach Your Children to Fear God

"For I have known him, in order that he may command his children and his household after him, that they keep the way of the LORD…" (Genesis 18:19).

In order to instruct our children effectively, it is not enough to merely communicate the truth to them, we must exemplify it. The apostle Paul instructed Timothy: "These things command and teach. Let no one despise your youth, but be an example to the believers in word, in conduct, in love, in spirit, in faith, in purity" (2 Timothy 4:11-12).

I have had the opportunity to visit many nations throughout the world and minister to prominent spiritual leaders, and I have been able to see firsthand the crisis that has come as a result of the lack of fatherly love. So many people need to be loved by a father, and now is the time that God has chosen to bring restoration to the father's love in families. The Heavenly Father's arms are stretched out wide to those who have not had that type of love, and He tells us: "You are not alone. I am here. Come and rest in My arms and let Me love you."

Every Family is Blessed by the Paternal Blessing

God is our true Father, and when we know Him, He fills the void that we feel. The apostle Paul stated: "Blessed be the God and Father of our Lord Jesus Christ, who has blessed us with every spiritual blessing in the heavenly places in Christ" (Ephesians 1:3). It states that the first blessing is the paternal blessing. The father should bless his children in the same manner in which we receive Father God's blessing. To bless means to release goodness and do well to your children. To curse means to speak ill and to release evil over your children. A father has the ability to curse his children with the words spoken over them. When the words express rejection, contempt, or vulgarity to the children, they are prophetic; they produce an effect in the spirit realm that transforms circumstances so that everything the father declares over them will come to pass.

We must comprehend that out of the more than six billion people who live in the world today, very few of them have been chosen to be part of God's family. You and I are included in that few—you are part of a royal family. You must learn how to live and behave as a prince, for you are a child of the King. That is why you must make an effort to learn the Word, minister, and learn the ways of God's Kingdom. You have been adopted as a child of God.

Jesus Called God, "Father"

The Lord Jesus introduced one of the most revolutionary doctrines of the age when He taught people to pray saying: "Our Father…"

Right up until that time no Jew had ever dared to call God "Father." The Israelites father was Abraham, and they were so proud to say: "Abraham is our father" (John 8:39a).

It was very dignifying for Jews to claim that Abraham was their father. Furthermore, for someone to affirm that God was their Father, was blasphemy because it signified that that person was placing himself or herself at the same level as God.

Can you imagine how offended the Sectarian Jews were when they heard Jesus confess: "God is my Father…the Father and I are one…I have come to do my Father's will." They were so upset that they came to believe He was pretentious, which was one of the reasons why they persecuted and accused Him of being a blasphemer. "For a good work we do not stone You, but for blasphemy, and because You, being a Man, make Yourself God" (John 10:33). To which He responded: "…do you say of Him whom the Father sanctified and sent into the world, 'You are blaspheming,' because I said, 'I am the Son of God?' If I do not do the works of My Father, do not believe Me; but if I do, though you do not believe Me, believe the works, that you may know and believe that the Father is in Me, and I in Him" (John 10:36-38).

Through Jesus We Can Call God, "Father"

Jesus was able to call God "Father," because He had His divine nature. In order for us to call God "Father," we must first be adopted as His child, which has been made possible through our faith in Jesus Christ. "But as many as received Him, to them He gave the right to become children of God, to those who believe in His name: who were born, not of blood, nor of the will of the flesh, nor of the will of man, but of God" (John 1:12-13).

You are a child of God, and a part of the royal family, so you must dress with robes that are worthy of being seen in God's palace. You must make an effort to learn and meditate on the Word, which teaches you the principles of the kingdom because you have been adopted as a child of God.

All who have believed in Jesus are able to call God, "Father," because:

- He gave us life while we were dead (see Ephesians 2:1).
- He opened our eyes to turn us from darkness to light, and from the power of Satan to God, that we may receive forgiveness of sins and an inheritance among those who are sanctified by faith (see Acts 26:18).
- He gave us the right to become children of God (see John 1:12).
- We have been crucified with Christ; we no longer live, but Christ lives in us (see Galatians 2:20).
- The Spirit of God guides us (see Romans 8:14).
- He made us partakers of His divine nature (see 2 Peter 1:4).

We Know the Father Through Jesus

God sees everything and His eyes watch over everything that exists under heaven, there is none like Him. He is the most loving and wonderful Father in the universe, and for this reason, the closest thing to His heart is a father's heart. No one can call God "Father" without first going through Jesus. Jesus was the One who removed the veil and opened the door so that we can come to the Heavenly Father. Only the person who has experienced the revelation of what Jesus bore for us on the Cross will be able to know God as their Father. Those who have not experienced or understood the sacrifice Jesus made on the Cross of Calvary will not be able to know God as their Father. Only when a person accepts Christ as their Lord and Savior will be able to receive the benefits of the Cross, which opens the path for them to relate to the Father.

If you are in need of medical attention, you get directions to the doctor's office. If you need to know God, you must know His address, and the only direction is through the Cross of Calvary. Why at Calvary's Cross? Because when you discover its power, you will leave failure behind and your life will be transformed into a blessed one. The Cross cancelled all curses, sickness was destroyed, and all darkness was dissipated. There is no other power like the Cross of Jesus Christ.

Knowing Jesus Signifies Knowing the Father

Before I was able to discover God as my Father, I first had to know Jesus of Nazareth. When I was spiritually blind, I told Him that if He really existed, I wanted to know Him.

I remember telling Him: "Jesus, I don't know You, but if You indeed are as real and powerful as the Bible claims You are, I want You to transform me right now and do something with my life."

I wanted the change to occur instantaneously, not a day later, and I thought: "If He is God, He can do it right now!" I said that quick prayer and I began to wait for the response. About fifteen minutes later, while staring at the front door, I witnessed an intense light that came straight towards me and stood beside me. I knew it was the presence of Jesus. I started to feel my entire body consumed with heat; it was like a ball of fire surrounding me.

For the first time in my life, I was convicted of sin. Prior to that moment, I had done no harm to anybody, so I believed that I was a good person, and I justified everything I had done in the past. Yet, while I was under that spotlight, I felt like the greatest sinner in the world. I was able to see myself through God's eyes and I felt Him pierce through to the deepest part of me where my sins were exposed in God's light. I had no idea how to break free from them, and I felt like the most unworthy and impure individual before His sight. I felt unworthy of His grace and love, the only thing I could do was tell Him: "Depart from me, for I am a sinner." But something real happened to me as I confessed all of my sins and began to give a detailed description of them. Later, I read what the apostle John said: "If we confess our sins, He is faithful and just to forgive us our sins and to cleanse us from all unrighteousness" (1 John 1:9).

My Father's Forgiveness

I never knew that I could go before the Lord with all my sins. I had confessed my sins to men many times before, but after the confessionals, my sins did not disappear, they were still there. That day I saw a hand literally penetrate through me from the top of my head to the sole of my feet. What seemed like the weight of the world had lifted off my shoulders and I became free of all oppression. For the very first time in my life, I felt my sins disappear and I knew what it felt like to be completely forgiven. The psalmist David said: "As far as the east is from the west, so far has He removed our transgressions from us" (Psalm 103:12). Since then, I have become fascinated with praying and reading the Word.

The next day, I tried to light up a cigarette, and the second I took a puff, my throat was in excruciating pain and I found that I could no longer stand to smoke. I had no other choice than to quit, even though I had smoked several cigarettes a day. I had the same experience with liquor and profanity, I could no longer stand the taste, and the only language that I knew was to worship and exalt the Lord.

Resting in the Father's Arms

The moment that God revealed Himself to me, I had no one that I can go to for guidance on how to nurture this new relationship. So I took a leap of faith and decided to talk to God. Every night I spent time conversing with Him. I often spoke to Him with fear in my heart because I had an erroneous impression of what He was like. I believed God to be extremely strict and severe in His dealings. I pictured Him sitting on the throne with a whip in His hand waiting for me to make a mistake, until the day I heard a voice tell me: "Who told you that God was like that? Don't you know that He has His arms stretched out to you, just waiting for you to run into His open arms and rest in Him?" What a major revelation I received at that moment. I was instantaneously impressed, and in an act of faith, I ran into His arms. I was in my bedroom with my lights turned off, but it felt as if my room lit up. I understood it was a sign from God that He had received me with an embrace. When I was ten years old, my father passed away and I grew up without the warmth, love, or affection of a father. Very few times was I able to see him while he was alive. But that particular day, every single emotional void in my life was filled and covered by God the Father.

I have witnessed so many lives restored as they take refuge in His loving arms, because He is real. Since people cannot see God, many times they come to believe that He has no active interest in them. Yet, when they overcome their fears and doubts, they are able to run into His open arms. By this act of faith, they discover that their Heavenly Father is real!

KNOWING THE POWER OF THE CROSS.

Jesus said: "I am the door. If anyone enters by Me, he will be saved, and will go in and out and find pasture" (John 10:9). Jesus is the Lamb of God that was sent to earth to carry our sins and iniquities upon His shoulders. Although He did not commit a single sin, the Father allowed Him to carry all the sins of mankind, thus becoming the sacrificial lamb who took our place so that we would not receive what we so rightfully deserved.

Although many people know that Christ died on the Cross, they have not yet had a revelation of the victory that came as a result of His death. Understanding this truth is the foundation of the Christian walk. This is also the fundamental principle for a prayer life. By no means is Christ's death a martyr's sacrifice, His death was for you and me. We should have been the ones who die there, yet, God in His great love for mankind, imposed our sins upon His Son.

Adam's Sin

How many sins have we committed? If Adam was thrown out of the garden because of one sin, what hope is there for us? None. Yet, Jesus carried our sins, and as we raise our eyes and contemplate Him hanging on the Cross and look close enough, you will see your face and mine reflected in His sacrifice. If we see our reflection there, we will understand that His death was our death. It will no longer be something that occurred in theory, but rather, an extraordinary experience that can only be acquired through faith. Many people have tried to grasp redemption through logic and have been left confused in their own concepts. The bottom line is that the entire Christian life is only accepted by faith and through faith.

Paul understood this concept and was able to say: "I have been crucified with Christ; it is no longer I who live, but Christ lives in me; and the life which I now live in the flesh I live by faith in the Son of God, who loved me and gave Himself for me" (Galatians 2:20). Paul lived the revelation of the Cross on a daily basis. To Paul, Christ's death was not merely just Christ's death, it was also his death. That is why Paul claimed: "Brothers, I die to self daily." The Cross was not just something he experienced the day of his conversion, it was something he experienced daily. He wrote to the Galatians saying: "And those who are Christ's have crucified the flesh with its passions and desires" (Galatians 5:24). As humans, we are subject to passions, and if we do not keep them under control, we will experience chaos. The only way to bring order to those passions is by receiving the victory of the Cross, where every disorderly passion is crucified.

The Apostle also declared: "…bringing every thought into captivity to the obedience of Christ" (2 Corinthians 10:5b). This tells us to surrender every thought and feeling at the foot of the Cross.

The Benefits of the Cross

As a man or woman of God who longs to relate to the Father, you must comprehend that you can only go to the Father through the Son. This is why you must die with Christ. When you die with Him, something great will occur in your life. You will discover that the Cross releases a flow of blessings that will touch your life and the lives of all who will come to the Cross as well.

The Power of the Blood

Believers must crucify their flesh, passions, desires, and feelings, and be cleansed by the blood of Jesus because: "…the blood of Jesus Christ His Son cleanses us from all sin" (1 John 1:7). This means that we must place ourselves at the foot of the Cross and ask the Lord: "Apply Your blood upon my life: wash me, cleanse me, and sanctify me."

You should not start your day without spending time alone with God and doing this.

Your prayer life is essential! Think about how much time this process takes. It takes me an hour and a half daily to do it the right way. If you desire to have a strong and steadfast leadership, your prayer life should be an intense, fervent, and disciplined experience. The moment you are cleansed by the blood of the Lamb, you become a participant of all the blessings that flow from the very throne of God.

Appropriate Your Salvation

Paul said that we should consider our salvation as a helmet that protects our head. Salvation is not a reward for good behavior, being merciful, or being a religious person. Salvation is a gift that God bestows to us. We must appropriate our salvation by filling our thoughts with faith, optimism, and hope. The enemy's darts come wrapped in human thoughts, and with them Satan tries to bring guilt. If he accomplishes this, your head is left unprotected. This is why we must fill our mind daily with the Word of God, so that it can help us experience growth and be victorious in our life for His glory.

Healing is For You

We always speak about healing with conviction, but when sickness attacks one of our family members, we start engaging in a great battle of faith. My wife suffered with a thyroid infection for twelve years. We proclaimed all of the healing promises found in God's Word, and we resisted medical intervention because we believed it would have been a sign that we lacked faith. Although the doctors claimed that surgery was our only hope, we resisted and awaiting the miracle, until God spoke to my wife in a dream and told her to have surgery. After this, the Lord convinced us that surgery was His will. After the surgery, we faced one of the most difficult trials of our lives, because her metabolism started decomposing. This caused us to strengthen ourselves in God and maintain a high level of faith. We later came to understand that when things like this occur, there is a great blessing in store. The Lord used this situation to show Claudia the revelation of the Cross, where she literally felt crucified with Christ. After this experience, just prior to going forward to share a teaching on a Sunday, Claudia told me: "I would rather someone else teach today, because I do not feel very well." I responded: "You have the Word. When you go forth to the platform, God's power will be over you and will renew your strength."

Confess That the Power of
the Blood Brings Forth Healing

As soon as my wife started to speak, the anointing descended upon the congregation. She then said: "I believe we have entered into an open war against hell, and only the courageous will engage in this war. Going to war means that you are willing to lose your life. A warrior knows that he may very well have to die. He will do it because he is committed to the cause. If he does not want to go, he still has the chance to stay back because this must be a voluntary act. I believe that this church is committed to face the powers of darkness in order to redeem this nation; it is a cause for which we must be willing to lose our lives. Even when difficulties arise, we must be committed one hundred percent to the Lord. Cowards will not inherit the Kingdom of Heaven, because they will stay roaming around in the desert for years. We who are courageous are able to confront the enemy. We will change the spiritual climate of this nation because David's anointing rests upon this church. God will use you to usher in the greatest revival history has ever recorded."

As we concentrate on the warriors, these should know the weapons of offense and defense to count on.

If you believe you are one of the courageous ones for the Lord, you must possess three important weapons:

1. The Blood of the Lamb

"And they overcame him by the blood of the Lamb and by the word of their testimony, and they did not love their lives to the death" (Revelation 12:11). You must give a face to every week of your life.

To this week, you can give it the face of the "revelation of the Cross" so that you can feel its effects. Ask the Holy Spirit to grant you that experience. How do we overcome evil? Evil is a person. In the same manner that good is represented in Jesus and in the Father, the enemy represents evil; he is the dragon or the serpent that is mentioned in the Bible. A fundamental principle of the revelation of the Cross is the power in the blood of Jesus. When the Israelites were delivered from slavery in Egypt, Moses did something very symbolic, which they called "Passover." They had to sacrifice a lamb, whose blood would be placed on the doorpost of their home. That lamb was representative of Jesus on the Cross of Calvary. Evil must depart from your life, family and your church when you experience the power of the blood.

2. The Revelation of the Word

In any situation you face, you must apply the scripture that relates to it. For example, if you are dealing with sickness: "... by His stripes we are healed." If you are in turmoil, declare:

"…the peace of God that surpasses all understanding." God's Word must dwell abundantly in our hearts. We must believe and act based on its truth. You will be able to conquer healing, prosperity, peace, wisdom, and anything else you are in need of.

3. The Power of Your Testimony

This relates to the confession of the Word. In an act of faith, you must confess that you are covered in the blood of Jesus and your sins are forgiven. If there are no arguments against you, evil will immediately depart from your home. In Revelation, John states that through the blood of Jesus we have been redeemed from the enemy's power. In ancient days, although evil lingered in the homes of the Egyptians, what was it that kept the angel of death from touching the Israelite's homes? The answer is the blood of the lamb they sacrificed in obedience, and with hyssop they took the blood and painted the doorposts. The revelation of the Cross is a spectacle of blood. You need to know the power found in the blood of Jesus. Wherever you are right now, I want you to feel the blood of the Son of God cover you from the crown of your head to the soles of your feet, and the forgiveness of your sins.

Two of the most powerful weapons that the enemy uses to attack Christians are guilt and condemnation for things we have done in the past or left undone. The book of Revelation teaches us that we have overcome by the power of our testimony of what the blood of Jesus has done for us. What is the marvelous work of the precious blood of Jesus? It is the cleansing of our sins and the payment of all of our debts.

His blood has powerfully redeemed us. The apostle Paul said: "For you know the grace of our Lord Jesus Christ, that though He was rich, yet for your sakes He became poor, that you through His poverty might become rich" (2 Corinthians 8:9). Jesus became poor so that others may be rich. We must submerge ourselves in the blood of the Lamb of God in order to purify our minds, thoughts and past. This will give us the warrior anointing to confront the Goliaths' in our nations.

I strongly believe that when John wrote: "...and they overcame him." He wrote it because of us. We have overcome the enemy because we know the power found in the blood of Jesus, and we understand the magnificence of God's Word. Yet, that blood is only powerful when we confess it with faith.

After Claudia had shared that word with the congregation, she led them in prayer confessing what the blood of Jesus had done for her, and her body was completely healed that day. The healing not only reached her, but the church members as well.

*"God, thank you that through Jesus, I am able
to call You "Father." Thank you for the privilege
of being Your child and for the inheritance I
am entitled to receive through the lineage of
Abraham. I am moved by the thought that You
chose to die on the Cross so that I may have
life and gain access to Your presence because
of Your sacrifice. I come before You longing to
appropriate what You did for me. I desire to be
a better father so that I can reach the goal You set
before me when You said that we must be perfect
fathers even as You are perfect. Today, I am able
to call upon Your precious blood and be cleansed.
I am able to confess that Jesus has forgiven my
sins, and has justified and sanctified me. Thanks
to Your blood, You can see me as sinless. I can
go to the Cross and lay down all my weaknesses
and receive Your healing, deliverance, peace, and
fullness of life. Thank you for filling the void
that my earthly parents left in me. You are a
loving and tender Father who is always willing
to help me. I pray that You open my spiritual eyes
so that I may be able to see all the blessings that
You have in store for me. In Jesus' name, Amen."*

Chapter 2

KNOWING THE GOD OF HEAVEN

"...In heaven..." (Matthew 6:9)

Wise King Solomon's prayer as he dedicated the Temple to God was: "But will God indeed dwell on the earth? Behold, heaven and the heaven of heavens cannot contain You. How much less this temple which I have built!" (1 Kings 8:27). With this prayer, which was inspired by the Holy Spirit, he confessed the existence of three heavens: the atmosphere, the stratosphere, and God's heaven (third heaven), where it was believed that Paul was transported when he went to paradise and heard words that no man on earth was able to utter or express.

When you think of heaven, how do you imagine it? Often when someone describes how wonderful something is, they say: "Ah, this is heaven!" One tends to compare heaven to a place where there would be no sadness, fear, pain, oppression, sickness or needs. Heaven is a place that is filled with happiness. Hell is the opposite of what heaven is. Hell contains affliction, bitterness, infidelity, jealousy, hate, grudges and misery. Hell represents a desolate place, and that is why we must truly understand that this is not what God has destined for His children. He desires to bless us.

The God we find in the Bible is a real and living God who is there to help you overcome your struggles, suffers when you are in need, and totally transforms lives. You were not born in this world to be alone, since He is the One who sent you. You can always count on His help and support.

The God of the Impossible

The Lord called Abraham when he was seventy-five years old. Abraham and his wife Sarah faced countless struggles. Their heart's desire was that God would give them the privilege of conceiving a child, which was absolutely impossible because Sarah was barren. Yet, God made a promise to them, they believed, and saw their circumstance completely transformed. They got to know God as the God of the impossible. The word impossible is not part of God's vocabulary. That is why Jesus said: "If you can believe, all things are possible to him who believes" (Mark 9:23). Abraham and Sarah chose not to look at their circumstances and had an intimate relationship with the God of heaven–the God of the impossible. Therefore, Abraham no longer looked at his situation the same way. He started to confess and tell everyone that he would be the father of multitudes.

The fact of the matter was that his wife was old and barren. Many believed that Abraham was delusional, yet he was not influenced by others. Abraham got to know the God of heaven through His promise. That word brought him into an intimate relationship with God, and Abraham did not get sidetracked from that promise; he did not look to the left or to the right. More than likely those who surrounded him said: "Abraham, get a grip on reality. How do you expect to have children if you and your wife are old?" The only thing he could envision was the miracle, because God had declared it to be. Through the eyes of faith, Abraham saw his descendants and called them into existence. He called things that were not as though they were, with the assurance that the God of the impossible and every word that God spoke has power and will come to pass in due time. He learned how to walk in the word God had given him. That word became life to his thoughts, and every night he would stimulate it when he looked at the stars with thanksgiving for the children that God would give him someday. Abraham knew that they would be as numerous as the stars in the heavens. He never listened to the voice of doubt or looked at his current circumstance.

The God of heaven is the One who responds to, and changes, impossible situations. He is a God who calls things that do not exist as things they do. He is a miracle working God who intimately relates to those who have faith. No matter what situation you may be going through today, He will not let you fight your battle alone. Rise up! The God of the impossible is on your side, move forward and conquer in the battle.

The God That Supplies All Your Needs

David got to know the God who always provides, that is why he wrote: "The Lord is my shepherd; I shall not want" (Psalm 23:1). One thing I have learned in life is that most of our difficulties are conceived in our minds; they do not come from God. He simply desires for us to run to Him and tell Him our needs so that He can supply them. I remember when my girls were in school, the teachers would give them a list of the materials and textbooks they would need for class that semester. When they came home from school, they would run to me, hug and kiss me, and hand me this list of requirements. They then would proceed to give me another hug, and run off to play. I was stunned by the long list of things that were required, but they did not have a care in the world because they knew that I would take care of it. The Lord wants us to do the same with Him: come to Him with total confidence in prayer, kiss His face, and give Him the list of all our needs. It does not bother God when we present our petitions before Him, as a matter of fact, He is ready to respond to each and every one of our needs.

In 1983, my wife Claudia and I experienced this firsthand when we grabbed our calendar, jotted down our needs, and began praying for them. We were dumbfounded to see how the Lord answered seventy percent of our requests in the span of one year. Throughout the following year, we saw how every single one of the needs written had been fulfilled.

Jesus Calls Him Blessed

The God of heaven is a compassionate and loving God who desires for us to experience true happiness. It is so important to note the words that Jesus spoke the first time He spoke to the multitudes: "Then He opened His mouth and taught them, saying: 'Blessed are the poor in spirit, for theirs is the kingdom of heaven'" (Matthew 5:2-3). "Blessed" ("happy", "fortunate") are the poor in spirit. Another version (NLT) states: "God blesses those who realize their need for him…"

In other words, blessed are those who have faith, because the Kingdom of God belongs to them. This shows us that the kingdom of heaven belongs to those who have faith, and you can have it today if you believe God with all your heart.

Open Your Spiritual Eyes

God's desire is for each one of His children to receive the ability to believe in Him in order for the impossible to become possible. Jesus expressed it this way: "And Jesus said, 'For judgment I have come into this world, that those who do not see may see and that those who see may be made blind'" (John 9:39). God opened Abraham and Sarah's spiritual eyes so that they would be able to see their descendants, which would be as numerous as the stars in the heavens and as the sands of the shore.

The Lord is pleased that through faith His children can conquer whatever they desire. Everything we need already exists in the spiritual realm, but has not been made manifest in the natural realm. Every one of the blessings that we long for will come to pass, but first we must open our spiritual eyes. As we get to know the Father's heart, through His son Jesus, our spiritual eyes will be opened, and our understanding will be enlightened so that we can attain every goal we set before us.

On a recent trip I made to Guatemala, I met a man whose testimony impressed me. An indigenous tribe that resides in Guatemala raised this gentleman. Although he learned how to read and write at the age of sixteen, God made him a very prosperous man. As he shared his testimony with me, I asked him how he had achieved so much success. His response stunned me, he said: "I asked God to give me the same wisdom He had given to King Solomon, and He opened my eyes and my understanding. I was able to see prosperity, and by faith, I was able to make it a reality for my family and I." Currently, he is the owner of eleven companies that God has given him. His goal is to own twelve corporations.

This testimony got my attention because this man is living proof that it is never too late to start. I saw in him more than a mere example of success. I witnessed the power of faith and divine grace in action working together in harmony. This gentleman reminded me of Sarah, who gave birth to Isaac after it was humanly impossible for her to conceive. He could have gone through life feeling sorry for himself for not having been given opportunities for a better life, but he chose to wholeheartedly believe God and take a leap of faith, and God backed him up in all that he did.

The enemy will always try to attack us with low self-esteem, bringing fear, condemnation and guilt to our lives because he knows that all of this will rob our faith, but you must resist the devil and he will flee (see James 4:7).

You must enter into a new dimension of faith which will enable you to see beyond your present circumstance. By this, you will prosper in every area of your life, and this is God's will for you!

Confess What You Believe

God desires for you to achieve success and excellence. For this, you must be able to call the things that are not as though they are and walk in the dimension of faith. If you accept the fact that you will always live in poverty; you will be poor, but if you renounce and repent with your whole heart God will forgive you and give you a rich life. Ask the Lord to reveal Himself to you as the God of abundance who gives you much more than you can ever imagine or need. Ask Him to open the floodgates of heaven so that He may shower you with His blessings and supply all your needs.

Your lips have the power and authority that God has given you. Everything that you declare in faith will cause the angelic forces to be activated on your behalf.

Knowing the God of Today

A couple of months ago a precious family chose to move to Florida and get connected with our church. My wife Claudia and I started to disciple them. We immediately realized how hurt this couple had been. We longed for them to comprehend that God's plan was to prosper them. We used different methods to explain this principle to them, but it was difficult for them to grasp it. When we would tell them that God desired to prosper them greatly, they thought we were exaggerating in order to make them feel good. When we told them that God wanted them to have an abundant life, they thought that could only occur in a distant future. One day while we were sharing the word with them, their eyes lit up as we explained to them that in Moses' days, the Lord proved Himself to be the great "I am." God could have revealed Himself to be: the great "I was," but the children of Israel would have proceeded to follow the God of the past. He could have said: "I will be," but this declaration would have them long for the God of the future. But what a blessing, God showed Himself to be the God of today, the One who is interested in meeting our needs right now. Many believe in the God of tomorrow, and this is why they are unable to see their dreams come true, because they feel God is distant from them today.

God is not merely the God of yesterday either. He is the God of today and He desires to bless, prosper, and exalt us today. He wants to heal you today. He longs to restore you today. He desires to meet your needs today. He longs to deliver you from all the chains that bind you today.

Jesus Brings Heaven Into Our Circumstances

Jesus died, rose again, and ascended to heaven to sit at the right hand of the Father. The veil of the temple was torn in two. He interceded and established a direct line of communication between heaven and earth. Through Jesus we are able to bring heaven down into our circumstances. We are able to bring God's abundance to our situations, and experience multitudes being added to our ministry. God called you into the ministry and desires to use you to transform lives, cities and nations. All you must do is believe God and call the multitudes. Satan will plant the seeds of spiritual barrenness, but God declares that from this day forward you will have fruit in abundance. You will have thousands of disciples because God's anointing already rests upon your life.

You must get to know the God of heaven. He is so powerful and able to transform every adverse situation. Do not wait until tomorrow. If you only believe, God can perform the miracle that you are in need of today. If you accept doubt, fear will come as a result. If you have made a negative confession, you must repent today. Believe that your God is the God of the impossible and your miracle will happen today.

Exercise Your Authority

The apostle Paul, which God allowed the privilege of visiting the third heaven, wrote to the Ephesians so that they could comprehend the authority that had been given through Christ Jesus. In prayer Paul cried out: "...that the God of our Lord Jesus Christ, the Father of glory, may give to you the spirit of wisdom and revelation in the knowledge of Him, the eyes of your understanding being enlightened; that you may know what is the hope of His calling, what are the riches of the glory of His inheritance in the saints" (Ephesians 1:17-18).

The Apostle longed for every believer to comprehend:
• The hope of His calling.
• The riches of His Glory.
• The inheritance that belongs to all the saints.

That extraordinary power that He has given us is the same, "...which He worked in Christ when He raised Him from the dead and seated Him at His right hand in the heavenly places, far above all principality and power and might and dominion, and every name that is named, not only in this age but also in that which is to come. And He put all things under His feet, and gave Him to be head over all things to the church, which is His body, the fullness of Him who fills all in all" (Ephesians 1:20-23).

The Father is seated in heaven and when Jesus resurrected, He was promoted to the same level of dignity as the Father. Prior to His coming to earth, Jesus was clothed in splendor and glory, but He chose to rid Himself of His divinity so that He may come to earth as a man. In this form, He suffered temptation, rejection, mocking, betrayal, and the death on the Cross. With this, He became victorious over every condition He had ever suffered or that we may ever suffer. On the third day after dying, the power of the Holy Spirit entered into Him to raise Him up in power. The following forty days, He appeared to His disciples giving them proof that He indeed was alive. With five hundred individuals to witness it, He ascended to heaven and sat down at the right hand of the Father. Majestically, He reigns and acquires a name that is above all names. At His name, every knee shall bow and every tongue will confess that Jesus Christ is Lord. "Heaven is My throne, and earth is My footstool. Where is the house that you will build Me? (Isaiah 66:1). Jesus came down from heaven to redeem the world, and redemption was conquered through His death on the Cross. God's power resurrected Him.

Jesus Raised Us Up With Authority

Through our faith in Jesus, we have been given the same level of authority as Him. The Bible declares: "...and raised us up together, and made us sit together in the heavenly places in Christ Jesus" (Ephesians 2:6). Although our feet may be planted on earth, our spiritual nature is seated in heaven, and all things have been submitted under His feet. We, as the body of Christ, understand that God has given us spiritual authority because we are His feet. The fact that some do not exercise their authority is mainly because they do not believe. If we see things from below, we tend to feel small; like a mere spec in the universe.

If we are able to look on things from on high, we will find that the highest mountain peak seems small in comparison to the face of the earth. If we take our rightful position in Christ, we will never be living under our circumstance, we will always be living above them.

Jesus said: "Behold, I give you the authority to trample on serpents and scorpions, and over all the power of the enemy, and nothing shall by any means hurt you" (Luke 10:19). He also declared: "...these signs will follow those who believe, in My name they will cast out demons; they will speak with new tongues; they will take up serpents; and if they drink anything deadly, it will by no means hurt them; they will lay hands on the sick, and they will recover" (Mark 16:17-18).

When I truly understood this revelation, the way in which I prayed changed drastically. I used to think the enemy was a giant and would take all my energy to tie him up and rebuke him. Once I truly grabbed a hold of the word, I no longer looked up at the enemy with fear, but understood that he was under my feet. I also understood that the Church is Jesus' feet. As Paul said: "…God placed all things under His feet and appointed Him to be head over everything for the church" (Ephesians 1:22). As the Church, we must exercise all the authority given to us so that we can unleash that power in our homes, churches and nations, and to set the captives free from oppression.

"Loving Father and holy God, thank you for Your goodness in transforming my nature and making me a new creation. Thank you Jesus, for conquering death and for being seated at the right hand of God. I am so thankful that You have accepted my faith and have given my life a spiritual nature, which was dead because of my sins. Thank you for the privilege You have given me to be seated in the heavenly places together with You. And although I am still walking on the earth in the natural, I am so grateful I can live above my circumstances exercising the authority You have given me over the forces of evil. Thank you for bringing down the blessings of heaven so that I may enjoy them with my family and disciples today. In Jesus' name, Amen."

Chapter 3

BENEFITS OF RECEIVING THE HOLINESS OF GOD

"...Hallowed be Your name..." (Matthew 6:9b)

Jesus exemplified God's character; He taught us to pray and call God "Father." Only those who truly have His character are able to call Him "Father." What enables us to participate in His divine character is the fact that we have come to know Him through His Son, Jesus Christ. The apostle John wrote: "No one has seen God at any time. The only begotten Son, who is in the bosom of the Father, He has declared Him" (John 1:18). One of Jesus' disciples, Philip, said to Him: "'Lord, show us the Father and that will be enough for us.' Jesus answered: 'Don't you know me, Philip, even after I have been among you such a long time? Anyone who has seen me has seen the Father. How can you say, 'Show us the Father?'" (John 14:8-9).

The Father and Jesus Are One

Before Jesus was betrayed by Judas, He prayed to His Father for His disciples: "…that they all may be one, as You, Father, are in Me, and I in You; that they also may be one in Us, that the world may believe that You sent Me" (John 17:21). Just as the Father and Jesus are one, we are now one in Christ and the Father, and we reflect the Father and the Son's character. Saying: "Hallowed be Your name," means that God is holy–that is His nature.

It is vital to understand that we are living in a crucial season in which we must walk with a firm conviction of the calling the Lord has placed upon our lives. In the spirit realm, evil forces are desperately battling to control the spiritual lives of individuals they desire to destroy. Just as the days of Elijah, God is raising up servants today who will restore His altar, bring us back to a heart of genuine worship so that God will be the only one true God (remove all other gods), and be determined to serve the most Holy God. In order to restore God's altar, we must:

1. Speak in the Name of the Lord (1 Kings 17:1b)

"And Elijah the Tishbite, of the inhabitants of Gilead, said to Ahab, 'As the LORD God of Israel lives, before whom I stand, there shall not be dew nor rain these years, except at my word.'" Elijah was not speaking for himself, he was speaking for God. Each one of us has a prophetic nature and as we prophesy with our lips, the words we pronounce become seeds. If we speak negatively, they become bad seeds. If we speak positively, they become good seeds. Proverbs states: "You are snared by the words of your mouth. You are taken by the words of your mouth" (Proverbs 6:2). Every word you pronounce will become your food. What you sow today through your words, will be the food you eat tomorrow. How do you envision your disciples in a couple of years? They will be the result of all that you have believed and spoken about them. You can only confess what you really believe in your heart.

Elijah was a man who understood the profound power of words. He also had the conviction that God had called him to restore the altar that the children of Israel had destroyed with profanity and deeds. The first one to exemplify this bad behavior in turning to other gods was the king and his entire entourage. Consequently, the Lord had to raise up Elijah in a time of apostasy, to confront the governing king and his people. Then, in a supernatural way, remove the veil that was blinding them from recognizing that the god the king worshipped, known as Baal, was a mere idol and not the one true and living God.

2. Restoring the Altar of God in Our Mind (1 Kings 18:21)

"And Elijah came to all the people, and said, 'How long will you falter between two opinions? If the LORD is God, follow Him; but if Baal, follow him.' But the people answered him not a word." Israel had departed from God and started to worship Baal (which means "lord"). They had another god that was not the God of Israel. All of God's prophets had been massacred and in their place were all the false prophets, witches, and sorcerers who had gained popularity because the people believed in them.

Idolatry is an abomination in God's eyes. God demands exclusivity. He cannot accept someone who worships Him and another god simultaneously. Some have allowed their hearts to be consumed with selfishness, which has resulted in a divided heart. They hear God's voice, as well as the voice of the enemy, and this causes inner conflict. Although the Lord is speaking clearly about what we are to do, soon afterwards the enemy's voice fills our minds with arguments, lying to us. Saying to us that if we are obedient to the voice of God, we stand the chance to lose many things, and thereby he seeks to separate us from our divine purpose.

When someone gives place to the devil in their thoughts, they are bound with fears, anxiety, anguish and frustration, robbing them of their vision. Satan always speaks through our thoughts trying to control us. The thought knocks on the door of our mind. When we open that door we are accepting the spirit that generated that thought. From the moment that we allow it in, the evil spirit behind that thought is also accepted. That spirit now resides in that individual and subtly begins to take over their life.

Elijah had to confront the people saying: "How long will you waver between two opinions?" You cannot serve two gods. You cannot have God on your mind on Sunday morning, and the rest of the week be a slave to your carnal desires. You need to saturate your mind with God's Word: "The plans of the diligent lead surely to plenty, but those of everyone who is hasty, surely to poverty" (Proverbs 21:5). You must believe and have the certainty that God desires to make you grow until you have a church of great multitudes. In this way, you will bless thousands of people. All thoughts of doubt, fear and failure, that you may have do not come from you, they come from the enemy. Therefore, you must learn to identify them and cast them out of your life.

3. Restoring God's Altar With the Proper Offering (1 Kings 18:33)

"And he put the wood in order, cut the bull in pieces, and laid it on the wood, and said, 'Fill four water pots with water, and pour it on the burnt sacrifice and on the wood.'" Elijah knew that if he were to bring the proper offering before the Lord, He would receive it and consume it with His fire. What offering are we placing on the altar of our worship? Paul said: "I beseech you therefore, brethren, by the mercies of God, that you present your bodies a living sacrifice, holy, acceptable to God, which is your reasonable service" (Romans 12:1). He desires to see our lives surrendered in sacrificial obedience on His altar. This implies that we yield our will to the desires of God's heart. Many who claim to be servants of the Lord are not, because in reality, they are not doing what He commands. They have offered their lives only with their lips, and not with actions. One of the greatest examples of obedience and surrender can be found in the life of Abraham. He was extremely pleased with his son Isaac–the promise he had waited for so long–yet when God asked him to sacrifice his dear son on the altar, Abraham did not even hesitate.

Elijah knew that God would consume the sacrifice, which is why he asked for fire from heaven to descend upon it. The prophets of Baal wanted to do the same, but they did not achieve it. Fire did not come down from heaven, nor was there any manifestation, because Baal was not God. When Elijah prayed, fire fell down from heaven and the sacrifice was consumed. This teaches us that if we unite our mind with God's thoughts, His fire will come down, take hold of our lives, and light a fire that will burn in us to bring salvation to our household, family, city and nation.

Restoration means to place our lives in order. The body is the temple of the Holy Spirit and you must understand that your life cannot be in chaos. Since you have accepted Jesus, your life is no longer your own, it is God's. Perhaps you have allowed things that are not pleasing to God in your life. Today you must take corrective action and bring it into God's order. You must bring your health, mind, emotion, spiritual life, family life, and ministry into order. Bring complete restoration of God's altar and you must also restore your relationship with Him. This means that you must restore your self-confidence. If you believe that you are insignificant, worthless, and a failure, then you must rescue your dignity. You must realize that you are very important to God and that He desires for you to be a confident person. You must also restore relationships within your family. What is the use of winning the world for Christ if you lose your own family? You must strive to have an exemplary family. You should also pray and invest time to restore those divided relationships within your family. As you do this, God will place a new priestly anointing upon your life.

4. Restore the Altar With Twelve Stones (1 Kings 18:31)
"And Elijah took twelve stones, according to the number of the tribes of the sons of Jacob, to whom the word of the

LORD had come, saying, 'Israel shall be your name.'" Forming your twelve is to acknowledge that God moves through a team. The number twelve represents government. God was able to pastor the entire world through the twelve tribes of Israel. Jesus was able to pastor the Church through the twelve apostles. Paul said: "...having been built on the foundation of the apostles and prophets, Jesus Christ   Himself being the chief cornerstone" (Ephesians 2:20). Now is the time for you to assemble and form your twelve. God has not called you to be a loose stone within His Church. He desires for you to be part of a twelve, and to form your own twelve as well. This is the best way to pastor others, because you are constantly aware of their needs.

5. Restore the Altar Through the
Revelation of the Cross (1 Kings 18:33)

"And he put the wood in order, cut the bull in pieces, and laid it on the wood, and said, 'Fill four water pots with water, and pour it on the burnt sacrifice and on the wood.'" The wood on the altar of the Cross–the Cross of Jesus–is composed of two beams. The vertical beam signifies looking up towards God, and the horizontal beam signifies looking towards the needs of others. The Cross tells us that there, in one day, every curse was broken. A man named Jesus took all our curses, all our failures, all our sicknesses, all our poverty and rebellion, and nailed them to the Cross where they were destroyed completely. To restore God's altar, it is fundamental that we live the revelation of the Cross.

Just as Elijah was obedient to God's direction, you must do the same. It was very difficult for Elijah to face a pagan culture, yet, he chose to be obedient and have faith in the Lord. Because of this, God answered by fire, accepted the sacrifice, consumed the wood, water, and everything else the prophet had offered Him. The Lord was pleased with that offering.

To restore God's fallen altar requires you to give your best.

We Can Worship Him in Spirit and in Truth

Jesus told the Samaritan woman: "But the hour is coming, and now is when the true worshipers will worship the Father in spirit and truth; for the Father is seeking such to worship Him. God is Spirit and those who worship Him must worship in spirit and truth" (John 4:23-24).

God's very nature is holy; in other words, completely devoid of evil. God's holiness cannot fellowship with anything that is evil in this world. God's creation exists with the sole purpose of glorifying Him. This worship is so important to God that He will not share it with anybody, not even the most anointed of His servants. Satan, seeing the splendor of the divine majesty, and the glory and praise directed solely to God, allowed envy to take root in his heart. Evil came when he wanted to take God's place in worship. For this reason, he was thrown out of heaven with all of the angels that he had deceived.

From that moment, his desire was to be worshipped at all cost. He went as far as to offer Jesus all the kingdoms of this world, saying: "...All this authority I will give You, and their glory; for this has been delivered to me, and I give it to whomever I wish. Therefore, if You will worship before me, all will be Yours" (Luke 4:6-7).

Jesus responded, saying: "Away with you, Satan! For it is written, 'You shall worship the LORD your God, and Him only you shall serve'" (Matthew 4:10). Although Satan desired worship, the Lord reminded him that He would not share His worship with anyone.

God's nature is holy, and no one who exists is equal to His holiness. Eliphaz, one of Job's friends, said: "If God puts no trust in His saints, and the heavens are not pure in His sight, how much less man, who is abominable and filthy, who drinks iniquity like water" (Job 15:15-16).

The prophet Isaiah said: "In the year that King Uzziah died, I saw the Lord seated on a throne, high and exalted, and the train of his robe filled the temple" (Isaiah 6:1).

God's holiness is supreme and there are some benefits that we receive from it:

1. Holiness Produces Harmony

God created the first couple in His likeness and made them holy. "Then God said, 'Let us make man in our image, according to our likeness'" (Genesis 1:26). In other words, He created them to have His very nature and character. The Lord blessed the first couple and made them participants of all His treasures by creating the universe for them. Men and women are the expression of God's divine character. God Himself created sex and gave it to the marriage for their enjoyment; this blessing is a part of God's holiness. Immorality is the opposite of holiness. Satan wants to destroy marriages, and ignite men and women with inordinate affections to distance them from their relationship with God and lose holiness, because without holiness, no one can be near God. When individuals respect the boundaries that God has established, there is joy, happiness and blessing. When they leave those divine boundaries, there is confusion, frustration and curse. Holiness brings harmony to a marriage.

2. Holiness Leads to Integrity

Another translation for the word "holiness" is "footprint." If you put an object in a specific place for a while, when you pick it up, you will notice that a mark (or footprint) was left in the place where the object had been. Something similar occurred with Moses after having been in God's presence for forty days. When he came down from the mountain, everyone saw how his face radiated God's glory to such a degree that a veil had to be placed on him. Seeing this reminded them all to live a life of holiness and integrity.

As we draw near to God through His son, Jesus, the same mark of Christ's character is reproduced in us. The apostle Paul declared that just as Christ was, so are we. You must have a life of integrity. This means that you must be submitted to His laws.

3. Holiness Produces Generosity

Our God is extremely generous. He is not greedy or cheap. God's holiness is fearless. For this reason, heaven cannot contain His holiness, His glory, and His presence. Everything He does comes from a huge, generous heart. When God created the first couple, He did not think of giving them just a few acres of land. He was so generous that He thought ahead to future generations, and although they were just a couple, God gave them authority to rule over all the earth. Every man and woman must have a generous heart. Generosity is a part of God's holiness because He gives freely without holding back.

You must possess a generous heart when giving to God. God tests His children to see how giving they are. Why was Abel's offering recorded in scripture? Because he gave without reservation, giving God the best. He did not give his leftovers. You must surprise God with your offerings. The person who is generous with God, is generous with his or her family.

4. Holiness Produces Happiness

Some people believe that being spiritual requires that you be introverted, shy, and isolated, but the happiest people in the world are usually the most holy people. Holiness has nothing to do with being mystical or super religious. Jesus was quite a normal and happy individual. He never had strange gestures. He mingled with people, and when He spoke, His words were authoritative. He simply said to demons: "Get out," and they would flee immediately. Jesus was a man full of joy and happiness.

In a home where a family walks in holiness, there is no bitterness, sadness, complaining or murmuring. Because of joy and happiness, God's presence is felt throughout the entire house. When holiness is in our lives we express joy and delight. Fear, doubt, anxiety, complaints, worry and murmuring, are all things that rob you of your joy. This is why you must let go of everything that is keeping you from experiencing true happiness, and keep the joy alive in your home.

5. Holiness Produces Purity

God teaches us in scripture that everything found in heaven is holy and pure. When John explains in Revelation, the vision he had of the throne of God, he states that everything in heaven bows down and worships God, saying: "Holy, Holy, Holy." Why is God's holiness mentioned three times? Because God is triune: Father, Son, and Holy Spirit. The angels are constantly crying out: "Holy, Holy, Holy is the Lord," and in this moment of worship, they remove their crowns and lay them down in the presence of God. This is the same thing that occurs when we are confronted with God's purity, majesty, and holiness; we lay down our ministries, titles, and recognitions at Jesus' feet. When we worship God's holiness, the spiritual atmosphere is transformed into an environment of peace, and divine glory fills the place.

When we are confronted with God's holiness, we surrender our entire heart to Him and our spirit is open to hear His voice. The apostle Paul said: "Or do you not know that your body is the temple of the Holy Spirit who is in you, whom you have from God, and you are not your own?" (1 Corinthians 6:19). God did not choose a particular building in which to live, instead He chose to dwell inside of you because you believed in Him. God lives inside of you and dwells in your thoughts, emotions, desires, decisions, words, and everything that you are. You are the temple of God and His holiness dwells within you. When God's character is reproduced in you, your life is full of harmony, integrity, generosity, purity, and great joy.

"Father, I draw near to You acknowledging that You are a most holy God that is surrounded by angels because Your dwelling place is holy. Lord, I choose to remove everything in my heart that is not pleasing to You. I long for my heart to be Your altar. I lay my life down at Your altar that I may serve and worship You. In the same way You gave Your Son Jesus, I surrender every area of my life to You today. I worship You with all of my strength. I have decided to build You an altar that pleases You. I commit to the G12 Vision so that the nations of the world may know You as a loving and holy God. Lord, I know that it is because of Your holiness that we can enjoy harmony in our homes, which produces security, happiness, purity, and helps us to express our appreciation with generosity. I love you, God! Amen."

Chapter 4

KNOWING THE KINGDOM OF GOD

". . . your kingdom come . . ." (Matthew 6:10)

From the beginning of His ministry, Jesus knew that He was coming to this world with the specific mission of establishing the Kingdom of God. This was the theme of His first public address: "The time is fulfilled and the kingdom of God is at hand. Repent and believe in the gospel" (Mark 1:15). After the fall of man, God promised redemption. Through it, human beings would be free from sin's slavery and Satan's control; they would be transplanted from the kingdom of darkness into the glorious kingdom of our heavenly Father. However, several thousand years passed until the fulfillment of that word. The only way redemption could ever happen was if the Son of God would become a man, and as a man, confront the tempter and defeat him. For that reason, the first thing Jesus said at the beginning of His ministry was: "the time is fulfilled..." What time was He referring to? We know that this was God's perfect time: the time for His Son to defeat the adversary on His own turf; the moment to bring His kingdom to this world. In spite of that, the enemy's strategy has always been to blind the eyes of believers so that they are not able to understand the promise, because without understanding, there is no appropriation of the promise. Without it, Christians would live under the mistaken impression that the Kingdom of God cannot be received here on earth, but only in heaven when they have left this world.

Jesus possessed two natures: a divine one and a human one. He was as much the Son of God as He was the Son of Man. Nevertheless, He set aside His divine nature and consented to live in a mortal body. Jesus, the Christ, brought the Kingdom of God to this world as a man and not in His divine condition. We know that He paid a very high price for it, but He did it so that the kingdom of darkness would not have any influence over any of those who have believed the gospel.

The only way in which man can take hold of the heavenly blessings is by acknowledging his own mistakes and making a decision to experience genuine repentance. Thus, he will turn his back on sin, his spiritual eyes will be opened, and he will realize that the Lord has already blessed us with every spiritual blessing in the heavenly places (see Ephesians 1:3).

"If you see the oppression of the poor and the violent perversion of justice and righteousness in a province, do not marvel at the matter; for high official watches over high official and higher officials are over them" (Ecclesiastes 5:8). When King Solomon makes this observation, he discerns that into the heart of man has entered a thirst for power and a lust for lording it over others, which breeds countless injustices.

He concludes by saying that there is someone who is above all; one who looks over each one of our actions. God is above all the kingdoms of this world where:

a.   The Kingdom of God is predominantly spiritual.
b.   The human kingdom is man's ability to fend for himself.

c. The animal kingdom is representative of survival.

d. The vegetable kingdom is representative of passivity.

e. The mineral kingdom is representative of unproductiveness.

Obviously, as people, we belong to the human kingdom, however, some people live depending on others in complete passivity, just like a vegetable. Others seem inanimate, totally unproductive, as if they were a mineral. But Jesus came to establish the Kingdom of God on this earth.

When Nicodemus went to talk with Jesus, He told him: "Most assuredly, I say to you, unless one is born again, he cannot see the kingdom of God" (John 3:3). With this, the Lord was saying that every person, without regard of religious status, must experience a new birth directly produced by the Holy Spirit who in turn takes man's faith and brings forth a spirit of life in him. As we accept Jesus as our Redeemer, God gives life to our spirit. From that moment on, we become spiritual beings residing in physical bodies. Through our senses, we make contact with the world around us; through our faith in Jesus Christ, we make contact with the Kingdom of God.

"Of His own will He brought us forth by the word of truth, that we may be a kind of firstfruits of His creatures" (James 1:18). The Lord left an open door so that everyone who believes in Him can experience the new birth.

Jesus said: ". . . unless a grain of wheat falls into the ground and dies, it remains alone; but if it dies, it produces much grain" (John 12:24). New birth implies a tearing away of our nature that has been affected by sin, so that the spirit of life may bear fruit in the spiritual kingdom.

"I will give you a new heart and put a new spirit within you; I will take the heart of stone out of your flesh and give you a heart of flesh. I will put My Spirit within you and cause you to walk in My statutes, and you will keep my judgments and do them" (Ezekiel 36:26-27).

In this manner, through the prophet, the Lord spoke of a new birth, without which no one will see the Kingdom of God.

When people met Jesus, they wanted to keep Him in their cities, but He would insist: "…I must preach the kingdom of God to the other cities also, because for this purpose I have been sent" (Luke 4:23). Thus, He would emphasize that one of the reasons He was in this world was to establish God's Kingdom in every corner of the earth and that the only way to accomplish it was through the preaching of the gospel.

"And Jesus went about all Galilee, teaching in their synagogues, preaching the gospel of the kingdom, and healing all kinds of sickness and all kinds of disease among the people" (Matthew 4:23). Matthew amplifies the way in which Jesus made an effort to establish the kingdom of God:

- Teaching in the synagogues.
- Preaching the gospel.
- Healing all kinds of sickness and diseases of the people.

The Lord knew that in order to make the gospel known, He had to preach it. I believe that today we have the same responsibility that the Lord had in those days: to preach the gospel of the Kingdom of God. To do so, it is very important to make use of all the media that technology makes available to us in order to effectively share the gospel that brings life to the whole world.

"No one can enter a strong man's house and plunder his goods, unless he first binds the strong man. And then he will plunder his house" (Mark 3:27). Jesus also came to destroy the works of the devil. The best way to do this is by binding the strong man, Satan, who for centuries has manipulated the human race. With the coming of Jesus to this world and His subsequent triumph on the Cross of Calvary, every stronghold on which Satan had placed his hope was completely torn down. Jesus paid a high price—His own blood—for the redemption of mankind.

Paul bears witness of how God entrusted to him the mission of preaching the gospel among the Gentiles. He summarizes it like this: "...to open their eyes, in order to turn them from darkness to light, and from the power of Satan to God, that they may receive forgiveness of sins and an inheritance among those who are sanctified..." (Acts 26:18). Paul knew that once people were able to understand the gospel, their spiritual eyes would be opened, they would no longer desire darkness, and having received light, they would not turn back. It is like when a person is blind and receives the miracle of sight, they no longer desire blindness, but rather, cling to the precious gift of sight.

GOD GAVE US THE KEYS TO THE KINGDOM

In order for the Church to work effectively, impacting the nations of the earth, it had to be equipped with the necessary tools. That is why Jesus took the time to provide His disciples with everything they would need while He was with them for three and a half years. Through personal contact, He shared with them His character, His vision, His compassion, His faith, and His full confidence in the Father. Shortly before leaving this world, He commanded them to not leave Jerusalem until they were endowed with power from on high. After Pentecost, all of their hearts were completely changed because they were all filled with the Holy Spirit–the third person of the trinity–who provided them the necessary assurance to begin their ministries.

The Lord told Peter: "And I will give you the keys of the kingdom of heaven . . ." (Matthew 16:19). This promise was fulfilled after the Apostle recognized, through divine inspiration, that Jesus was the Christ, the Son of the living God. Peter came to the realization that Jesus would take his place and die on the Cross of Calvary for him. As a result of this revelation, the Lord decided to change his name from Simon to Peter.

Later on, He asserts that, based on Peter's confession that Jesus is the Christ, on that foundation the Church would be built and the gates of hell would not prevail against it. After this transforming epiphany, the Lord tells him that He would give him the keys of the kingdom. But, what keys was He referring to? The same keys that Jesus used while He was in this world. These are the same keys you and I must use:

1. *The Key to the Preaching of the Word*

Peter was the first to open the Kingdom of Heaven with this key when he preached on the day of Pentecost and three thousand were converted. He also used the key when he preached later on at Cornelius' house, marking the beginning of the Gentile church (since these people were not Jews). It is God's desire that each one of us learn to use the power of the preaching of the Word. Paul wrote: "For the kingdom of God is not in word but in power" (1 Corinthians 4:20).

When we use His pure and faithful Word, God accomplishes extraordinary things. "So shall My Word be that goes forth from My mouth; it shall not return to Me void, but it shall accomplish what I please, and it shall prosper in the thing for which I sent it" (Isaiah 55:11). When the Word of God is preached under the anointing of the Holy Spirit, it is backed by signs and wonders. Through it, people feel the conviction of sin, which causes them to surrender their hearts before the love and compassion of Jesus. When Jesus sent His disciples to preach, He told them: "Heal the sick, cleanse the lepers, and raise the dead . . ." (Matthew 10:8). This teaches us the way in which He commissioned them to preach the gospel. There is no other way to transform families and cities except through the preaching of the Word. It creates an environment that brings the glory of God. That is why when a place is saturated with the Word, an angelic presence will be evident. The preacher is like a watchman who has the ability to see danger and warn the people so they will not be harmed.

We have the medicine that people need to cure the wounds of their soul and body. We have the most effective family protection policy. In addition, we have the restoring anointing that is capable of making the hearts of the fathers turn to the sons and the hearts of the sons turn to the fathers. We have an anointing capable of making spouses end their mutual offenses and decide to forgive each other, while living under God's peace and blessing.

"This book of the law shall not depart from your mouth, but you shall meditate in it day and night, that you may observe to do according to all that is written in it. For then you will make your way prosperous, and then you will have good success" (Joshua 1:8).

When the Word of God dwells in our hearts, it will be easy to talk about it, because a fire will be lit within us and nothing will be able to quench it. The only way to satisfy our hearts will be to make every effort to strategically and effectively preach the gospel.

2. The Key to See the Spiritual Realm

You must understand that in the physical world we make contact through our sight, but in the spiritual world we make contact through our faith. Jesus said: "The lamp of the body is the eye. If therefore your eye is good, your whole body will be full of light. But if your eye is bad, your whole body will be full of darkness" (Matthew 6:22-23). He was referring to spiritual vision. God has given you spiritual eyes so you can see His kingdom, but you must exercise this vision. Though the physical sight will try to blur the spiritual sight, the Lord has given you the capacity to see the kingdom of heaven. God is Spirit, and it is only through faith that you will be able to see the things which pertain to His spiritual kingdom.

It is there where you will be able to see the miracles you need: the physical healings, the restoring of families, and the development of your ministry. I have had the opportunity to attend meetings with thousands of people. Many times the Lord has given me visions in which I see bodies healed, minds freed, finances provided; and as I release the Word, of that which God desires to do, miracles take place in an indescribable way. You are not a second class believer! You are a child of God, born through faith and conceived by the Holy Spirit of God. The same nature that was at work in Jesus is at work in you, and the same power that indwelt Jesus, also dwells in you. Therefore, you can see what you desire through the eyes of faith. You simply have to take the step and ask the Holy Spirit to help you see His kingdom, the miracles, the healing, the provision and the multitudes.

At the beginning of my ministry, I never took time to dream, because my leaders had never taught me how. Because of this, their churches were small. They thought they could only grow to where their own intellectual abilities allowed. But one day, God took me to the beach in Colombia and told me to look at the sand on the seashore and told me that my descendants would be as numerous as the sand in the sea. I believed that word and began to see the multitudes. I saw how every grain of sand became a person. I saw hundreds of thousands of people. The Holy Spirit asked me: "What do you see?" And I answered: "I see hundreds of thousands of people." Then the Lord added: "I will give you this and more if you remain in My perfect will."

One of the greatest problems we need to resolve is the fact that we do not know how to dream. Our vision is obstructed because of what we have lived through or because of our natural circumstances, but God wants to turn us into dreamers.

The Lord told the prophet: "Then you shall see and become radiant..." (Isaiah 60:5a). If you do not see, you cannot be radiant; you must see in order to be radiant. When your spiritual eyes are opened, you can see the Holy Spirit's vision in the spiritual realm, and that what God has for you is good, pleasing and perfect. He can supply all of your emotional, physical, family and even ministerial needs. The Lord continues to say in Isaiah: "And your heart shall swell with joy; because the abundance of the sea shall be turned to you..." (Isaiah 60:5b).

You can do the same today. Contemplate the sand on the seashore and it will transform into people. When you are able to see them, it is because you have conceived them through visualization. It is through the proclamation of the Word that you will be able to call them and bring them forth.

You too can enter into the world of spiritual dreams and visions, but this is only accomplished through faith.

3. The Key of the Anointing That Turns Weakness Into Strength

When baby sharks are placed into a tank, their growth is so severely stunted that they reach adulthood measuring only a few centimeters. But if you take those same sharks out to the ocean, they will regain their normal size in a short amount of time. The same happens with the person who is born of the Spirit.

Maybe life has dealt you its share of hard knocks. Perhaps they have placed limits on your potential for accomplishments and you have yet to understand the Kingdom of God. But when you are born of the Spirit, you'll quickly begin to grow and develop; all because you have been born of the Spirit in power and faith. You must be born of God. The writer of the letter to the Hebrews, asserts that men of old: "…through faith subdued kingdoms, worked righteousness, obtained promises, stopped the mouths of lions, quenched the violence of fire, escaped the edge of the sword, out of weakness were made strong, became valiant in battle, turned to flight the armies of the aliens" (Hebrews 11:33-34). It seemed as though they would not make it, but they did with God's help.

How do you explain that Moses could stand before the most powerful man on earth (Pharaoh) and defeat him without a weapon—with only the authority of the Word—and then cause Pharaoh's whole army to perish under his authority? The answer is: he drew strength in the midst of his weakness. Do not allow problems to overwhelm you, nor let difficult circumstances make you believe you are worthless. Stand up like a conqueror. God wants to make a warrior and a conqueror out of you, but you must have faith. He wants to transform your weakness into strength. Isaiah said that the least of you will become a thousand, and the smallest, a mighty nation (see Isaiah 60:22). If you feel small, the Lord will give you a thousand!

4. The Key of Spiritual Authority

From now on, you must begin to behave according to your new nature. Do not behave like a failure or a coward. Behave like a man or woman of God.

The apostle Paul tells the Romans: "…who contrary to hope, in hope believed, so that he became the father of many nations, according to what was spoken, 'so shall your descendants be.' And not being weak in faith, he did not consider his own body, already dead (since he was about a hundred years old), and the deadness of Sarah's womb. He did not waver at the promise of God through unbelief, but was strengthened in faith, giving glory to God, and being fully convinced that what He had promised, He was also able to perform" (Romans 4:18-21).

People will try to make you see yourself in the natural, but God wants you to act according to the spiritual. You must see everything according to the spiritual realm.

When you are able to connect with God's world, you will begin to behave according to what you have received.

The analogy is like that of a pregnant woman who speaks of her child as though she already had him, because she feels him within her. The same occurs when we have conceived a miracle: you behave as though you have already received it. That which you are able to envision and conceive in your heart will be reflected in your behavior. Believe that through your faith, you will conquer the miracle need.

"My Lord, thank you for granting us Your kingdom. By faith, we take hold of all Your promises. Thank you, because Your kingdom has given life to my soul; my eyes are now open and I can behold the wonders of Your law. I know that everything I desire, You already have in the spiritual realm and that by faith I bring it into the natural realm. Thank you for the anointing I have to proclaim Your truth to those who do not yet know You. Lord, I declare that I have the strength that will cause me to do great things for You and that in Your name, all of my weaknesses become strengths. Today, I feel like an ambassador for the Kingdom of Heaven, for I know that hosts of angels are with me to back me up in everything I have to do. This I declare in the name of Jesus, Amen."

Chapter 5

KNOWING THE WILL OF GOD

". . . Your will be done on earth as it is in heaven . . ." (Matthew 6:10)

The angels obey the will of God. They immediately supply anything He desires, and do not object, argue or apologize, they just act. Those who touch the Father's heart are those who come to know and obey His will without question. The Psalmist declared: "Teach me to do Your will..." (Psalm 143:10).

God Reveals His Will to His Children

It is necessary to receive instructions from God in order to know His will for our lives. What you want to do for God is not important, but rather, what God wants you to do for Him. Many people are in God's work but not in His purpose. It is for this reason that you must be sensitive enough to discern God's will for your life. The blessing will come from the moment we make the decision to serve Jesus Christ with all of our hearts. For this, we must be conscious of whether or not we are fulfilling God's purpose on this earth. If He were to permit everyone to spend just a few minutes in hell, they would never be the same again. A deep compassion for the lost would spring up in their hearts; they would rush to rescue souls from the enemy's claws and from the depths of hell, and bring them into the Kingdom of God instead.

WHAT GOD CAN DO IN A SINGLE MINUTE..

John was at home one afternoon, bewildered, confused and depressed. He was completely overwhelmed by life's circumstances. His self-esteem, marriage, finances, work, and everything else seemed to be hopeless. He decided that this would be his last day. He planned an outing for his wife and kids, and sent them to a boy scouts meeting. Later on, he showered and got dressed for his own funeral.

After shaving, he searched around for a white nylon rope which he would use to make a noose. Then, he proceeded out the door in search of a tree limb on which to hang himself. A cell leader, who had risen to the challenge of winning one soul a week for Christ–and for a year and a half had trusted God to make him a soul-winner–was scheduled that day to follow up on a visitation card. He had faith that this could be the opportunity of the week to win a person for Christ.

He arrived at John's house, as he was searching for the tree limb. Oblivious to John's situation, he invited him to get into the car to go to the cell group meeting. John hesitantly agreed.

The cell leader asked John if he wanted to accept Jesus as his personal Savior and even before getting out of the car, the miracle of salvation took place. God had helped him to save this man's life and to win a soul. Later on, John shared that if this brother had arrived five minutes later, he would have been hanging from a tree. That same weekend John attended a Men's Encounter. He was set free and filled with the Holy Spirit. On that Sunday, John shared his testimony, and his wife came running to the platform with her eyes filled with tears. As she hugged him, she thanked God for saving her husband's life, her marriage, and her family. Today, God is blessing their marriage, finances and everything else. John and his wife were recently baptized and are already attending the School of Leaders.

God's will is that no one should perish but that all should come to repentance. It does not matter how close they are to perdition. All it takes is someone willing to go with the message of hope and allow God to do His extraordinary work. The Lord did this with Jonah when He sent him to Nineveh to warn the people; they were all saved because of his preaching.

God Gave Me a Second Chance

Years ago I was a victim of an attack carried out by a man possessed by demons. I was on my way to preach in the small church where I was pastoring. I was walking on a dark street, when a tall man approached me, placed his left hand over my chest and pressed me against his body. In his right hand he carried a long knife, which he inserted into the hand with which I held my Bible. He severed two of my fingers. In one he cut a tendon, and in the other he cut an artery. He then proceeded to stab my chest, and he nicked my heart. Due to the amount of blood clotting around my valves, I suffered an immediate cardiac arrest.

In mere seconds, my whole life flashed before me. It was one of the most distressing moments of my life. I thought

I had my whole life before me and refused to accept the circumstances that I was experiencing. I thought about my wife, who was a very young woman (she may have been eighteen then), and my daughter, Johanna, who was only 20 days old. I thought about the things I had accomplished, but also about the things I had yet to do for God. I realized that my work for Him on this earth had not been the best.

I was able to run for a block, and as I ran, my life flashed before me. This distressed me even more because I knew that my work on this earth was unfinished. I then collapsed at the end of the block. I had neither pulse nor breath. My heart had stopped; I was dead for thirty seconds, but my spiritual being did not fall, and this gruesome scene vanished as I saw the angels. Peace, joy, and tranquility came as I witnessed thousands of angels making circles above and below each other. There were circles of twenty, thirty and so on; a small circle and a large circle from high above to well below me. I was in the middle so I was not able see where it began or where it ended; it was a kind of angelic tunnel. All the angels sang a hymn of praise to God but I could not understand their language. With each melody that poured forth from their lips, joy increased in my heart until the joy was unspeakable.

After a while, I looked intently at the angels. I saw their long hair, their radiant countenance, their dark eyes, and their long robes. As I looked up I thought that at the end of that angelic tunnel I would find God. At that moment I felt great distress. I thought: "Lord, how can I come before You with empty hands? I have done nothing for You." From the depth of my soul, I wished for a second chance, since what I had done for the Kingdom of God was not enough. I could not present myself before Him with only fifty souls won during the time I was in ministry. So I said: "Lord, it is not possible for You to permit this death. It is an attack from the devil; he wants to shorten my life. I beg you Lord, that just as You defeated death and rose from the dead, give me the power to overcome it in Your name." When I finished praying, I opened my eyes as I came back to my body. The Lord allowed me to be away from my body for thirty minutes so that I could feel compassion for those who are lost.

My desire was not only for my country to come to know Him, but also to see entire nations transformed by the power of Jesus Christ. I know that the answer this world needs is found in Jesus of Nazareth. Jesus Christ is the only One with the answer to the current needs of the world.

God Has a Pre-ordained Destiny

After that experience, no one could explain why I had to undergo such adversity, but to me, it was one of the greatest experiences I ever had. After being stoned and left for dead by his adversaries, Paul had the privilege of being taken to the third heaven where God allowed him to see and hear things that no other human being has seen or heard. This experience so enriched him, that later on, the apostle remarks that he boasts of the man who had that experience.

When God allows us to see the spiritual kingdom, we are never the same, since we realize that we possess a spiritual nature which is both real and everlasting. This knowledge increases our responsibility to take the gospel to other people. I understood that the time we have in this world is very short, and that we must take full advantage of it. After that experience, I was able to comprehend the value of each soul. What the Bible teaches about salvation and condemnation is true. Our duty is to make an effort to become instruments in the hands of God to bring salvation to many. The Psalmist expressed: "Teach me to do Your will, for You are my God; Your Spirit is good. Lead me in the land of uprightness" (Psalm 143:10).

The Psalmist did not want to pass through this world unnoticed. He knew that he needed to be in the center of the divine will, so he asks for the Holy Spirit's direction. That is precisely what each one of us must do. We need to allow the Spirit of God to direct our paths. David said: "I delight to do Your will, O my God, and Your law is within my heart" (Psalm 40:8). When you do the will of God, you are satisfied. It is indescribable, because you know you are in the center of His will. This becomes a wall of protection that the Lord places around your life.

In one of the occasions when the Lord was hungry, His disciples went to buy Him food, and when they came back, they found the Lord speaking to a Samaritan woman. He saw them and said: "My food is to do the will of my Father."

Notice that for the Lord, the will of God was equivalent with what was most important in His life. No physical need or challenging test was strong enough to separate Him from the will of the Father.

Obedience: Refuge to Withstand the Test

When Jesus was about to be betrayed, He told His disciples: "Can you drink the cup I am going to drink?" (Matthew 20:22). This referred to if they could endure the suffering He was about to endure. Jesus was willing to give it all in obedience to the Father. He said: "O my Father, if this cup cannot pass away from Me unless I drink it, Your will be done" (Matthew 26:42). No one in this world, no matter how godly, wants to undergo suffering. No one wants to drink the cup of sickness, oppression or a broken home. Neither did Jesus want to go through pain and affliction, yet before His own will, was that of the Father. When you understand that God sometimes uses suffering to bring about great blessing, it helps you withstand each test with patience and love. We must be able to discern when a test is an attack of the enemy or when it is a tool that God is using to help us mature. So we must understand that to do His will implies withstanding all kinds of trials, as well as preparation. "And the servant who knew his master's will, and did not prepare himself or do according to his will, shall be beaten with many stripes" (Luke 12:47). Some people know what they have to do for God, however, they procrastinate or postpone it. These people, the Word says, will be beaten with many stripes. Let us imitate the servant in the parable of the talents, the one of whom the Lord said: "Well done, good and faithful servant..." (Matthew 25:21).

Obedience Leads to Brokenness

"For as the rain comes down and the snow from heaven, and does not return there, but waters the earth, and makes it bring forth and bud, that it may give seed to the sower, and bread to the eater; so shall My word be that goes forth from My mouth; it shall not return to Me void, but it shall accomplish what I please, and it shall prosper in the thing for which I sent it" (Isaiah 55:10-11). Everything that exists in the universe obeys the will of God.

When the Lord commissions the rain to water the earth, it does not argue back that it is depressed or has a cold, or that today it does not feel like working; it simply obeys the voice of God. If it were to not obey, we would have no food, and worldwide chaos.

Let us explore four transcendental aspects of how rain obeys the voice of God. These aspects are intricately linked with the steps toward the Vision.

1. The importance of winning souls
- The rain waters the earth -

For our purpose, the first stage of rain will represent "winning." We can never go beyond that which our faith will allow. Elijah predicted that it would not rain on the earth until he gave the word, and for three and a half years it did not rain in Israel. We conclude then, that if there is no rain, there is a drought. If there are no goals in soul winning, there will be no fruit of salvation. Let us not be afraid to work with discipleship goals. Establish clear and specific goals of how many people you want to win, and this will help you reach God's purpose. Everyone must establish goals. If you find yourself not reaching them, do not grow weary. Remember that when the Word of God is sent out, it will not return void; it will accomplish its purpose. A while ago, I left Bogotá for a few months, and the pastors there had set goals for themselves. When I returned, I found their spirits very low. They did not have the strength to win and it seemed as though they had weakened in their faith. They thought their goals were too large and began comparing themselves with other ministries.

When they spoke, they made excuses for why they could not fulfill them. It was the same story all around. At once, I was able to identify a spirit of unbelief that was robbing them of their faith, and I was able to discern that it was coming from one of the pastors who had been filled with fear. Through this pastor's confession, this spirit had reproduced itself in others. I confronted the pastor, brought him through to repentance, and to renouncing his sin. Then I ministered freedom to all of them and once again released a word of faith, and encouraged them to reach their goals. By the end of the year, they had reached all of their goals. The Word says that everything you declare will come to pass. When you speak, you become bound to your words. If you are doing the will of God, heaven will work on your behalf. Seize that spirit of conquest and tear down every argument of unbelief.

2. The Power of Encounters
-Rain Causes the Seed to Sprout-

It is necessary for the rain to deeply penetrate and loosen the earth. The process of taking seed and working with it is a process of brokenness, which we call: Consolidation. We take every person that comes to know the Lord to a three day retreat, so that they may experience the revelation of the Cross, receive the power of God, and go through a process of brokenness. Brokenness is an internal detachment from that which is external.

God has several ways to break a person: through sickness, financial crisis, a spouse, a boss or when a person willingly comes to the Cross and allows God to break them. Which one would you choose? The devil does not want us to understand the power of the Cross. He knows that when we do, he will no longer be able to deceive us because we will recognize his attacks, and rebuke him in Jesus' name.

The Cross of Jesus is as powerfully effective today as it was two thousand years ago. In it resides all the power of freedom. When you come to the Cross and crucify your sinful nature, the Lord provides you with a holy nature. We all know that the fruit is inside the seed. If the seed is not sown, it will remain a simple grain; but when it is sown, the external dies and the internal flourishes. When you come to the Cross, your ego and that which is external dies. There are those who do not want to fully die. They know that there are things they must leave behind, but they are not willing to do it. Just like the girl who had a kitten she loved dearly because he was her companion. One day the kitten died and the crying girl asked her dad, "What should we do with the kitten? I do not want it to be buried." Her dad explained that it must be done, and the girl replied, "Daddy, can we bury him in the garden and leave his tail above ground?"

Many want this kind of breaking. They ask the Lord to transform their lives, but not to intervene with certain areas. You must die completely, in order to fully enjoy the blessing.

3. Making Disciples
-Rain Causes the Earth to Spring Forth-

The function of rain is to spread the grain, break it up, and make fruit spring forth–thirty, sixty and a hundred-fold. This step is: Discipleship. We cannot remain satisfied living a traditional Christian life since a grain, no matter how beautiful, will remain just a grain if it stays in the storehouse. But if it is sown, it will bear much fruit.

Our goal should be to go through the breaking process where we will learn to have victory over adversity. If the Lord is breaking you, it is because He plans to give you abundant fruit. All the capacity to bear fruit is inside of you. This is where thirty, sixty and even hundred-fold grain comes from. That is, 12, 144, and 1728. As a pastor, one of my goals has always been to make a leader of every member of my church. Thanks to the process that is developed within the Vision, we have managed to effectively implement this in our ministry.

4. The Importance of Being Sent
-The Earth Gives Forth Abundant Fruit-

This is the step we know as sending. The rain has accomplished its goal, and now the fields can be harvested. Something similar happens within the Vision. Those twelve people who were mentored by you, are now ready to give fruit. This is when we see multiplication. God's will is that no one would perish, but that all would come to repentance. God's will for your life is to win souls, disciple them, and send them out to reach others. This work is not only reserved for pastors.

If you want to remain a beautiful grain in the storehouse, you will never receive your reward. If instead, you are a grain in God's garden, you must bear abundant fruit. The Lord does not want a church full of grain that refuses to die. There are all kinds of riches and potential inside of you. Maybe you have not been fruitful in certain areas, but God wants you to be fruitful in His work. Perhaps you think you are small and insignificant, but the Lord says that a little one shall become a thousand, and a small one, a strong nation (see Isaiah 60:22). Satan will tell you that there is too much sin in your life and that you cannot be fruitful for God, but you must remember that all your sins were forgiven and washed away by the blood of Jesus. Satan will want to make you feel miserable in order to drain your strength for victory, but you must rise up in power. He cannot steal your souls.

You are a servant of God, a child of God; therefore, you have His anointing and support. Get up and conquer the multitudes. God will give you many souls if you only believe. You must make the decision to serve Him with all your soul and strength.

Obedience Encourages Us to Evangelize

The Lord Jesus Christ taught: "This is the will of the Father who sent Me, that of all He has given Me I should lose nothing, but should raise it up at the last day" (John 6:39). What prompted Jesus to leave His throne in glory and to set aside His divine nature to become a man? It was His love for a world that is totally lost. He gave us a lesson in love and mercy when He left everything to come and save us, knowing that the price to pay would be His own blood. "Knowing that you were not redeemed with corruptible things, like silver or gold, from your aimless conduct received by tradition from your fathers, but with the precious blood of Christ, as of a lamb without blemish and without spot" (1 Peter 1:18-19).

Knowing the will of God is like having a multifaceted diamond; the one that shines the brightest is the one that motivates us to seek and save the lost. If that is the will of God, your duty and mine is to prepare ourselves and be diligent in our commission.

Paul said: "For if I preach the gospel, I have nothing to boast of, for necessity is laid upon me; yes, woe is me if I do not preach the gospel! For though I am free from all men, I have made myself a servant to all, that I might win the more; and to the Jews I became as a Jew that I might win Jews; to those who are under the law, as under the law, that I might win those who are under the law; to those who are without law, as without law (not being without law toward God, but under law toward Christ), that I might win those who are without law; to the weak I became as weak, that I might win the weak. I have become all things to all men, that I might by all means save some" (1 Corinthians 9:16,19-22).

If you want to do the will of God, you must become one who spreads the gospel. It is of the utmost importance that you meet the following criteria:

- You must have been redeemed.
- You must be biblically trained.
- You must have great compassion for the lost.
- You must be filled with the Holy Spirit.
- You must be an active member of a Christian church.
- You must have an amazing testimony.
- You must witness to others of what Christ has done in your life.

"Lord, what my heart longs for is to be in the center of Your will. Forgive me for all the times when I tried to follow my own desires. Forgive me for the times that I was blind to the blessings You had in store for me. I had let them pass me by. Lord, I have purposed to serve You with all of my being. I pray that You will help me to live daily in the center of Your will. I want to surrender my will and desires to Your Lordship. Help me feel the beating of Your heart so that I may have Your compassion for those who do not yet know You; and help me strive to bring them the message of hope and encouragement that they need. I ask this in the name of Jesus, Amen."

Chapter 6

THE PROVISION OF GOD FOR YOUR LIFE

"Give us this day our daily bread."
(Matthew 6:11)

It is incredible to see what God has in store for His children. His blessings go beyond what we can imagine. God wants to bless our whole being: our spirit, our soul and our bodies. He wants to provide for each one of our needs. However, lots of people have a battle in their minds because they do not believe that God can supply all their needs. They think that in order to prosper, they have to work really hard. They do not understand that prosperity was already conquered on the Cross, and that all they have to do is open their eyes to see it and appropriate God's riches.

Satan tries to make you blind to God's riches because he delights to see God's children in poverty. But when the spiritual eyes of the children of God are open and they realize that the enemy has deceived them for a long time, they must decide to cancel the adversary's arguments and believe in God's promises.

"Then God said, 'Let us make man in our image, according to our likeness; let them have dominion over the fish of the sea, over the birds of the air, and over the cattle, over all the earth and over every creeping thing that creeps on the earth.' So God created man in His own image; in the image of God He created him; male and female He created them. Then God blessed them, and God said to them, 'Be fruitful and multiply; fill the earth and subdue it; have dominion over the fish of the sea over the birds of the air, and over every living thing that moves on the earth'" (Genesis 1:26-28).

In this passage we can see that God, before creating man meticulously, worked on the place where he was to live. "The earth was without form, and void; and darkness was on the face of the deep. And the Spirit of God was hovering over the face of the waters" (Genesis 1:2). Before God started the process of creation, everything in this world was chaotic. He, however, transformed it into something beautiful. It is interesting to note that the Spirit of God hovered over the face of the waters. This helps us understand that God can transform a chaotic, adverse and difficult situation into a great paradise.

The enemy has managed to convince many people that they should accept a life of poverty and slavery. But the truth is that God has saved the best blessings for His children, and He has no second class children. If you understand these principles, your way of thinking will change, your faith will increase, and you will prosper because this is God's desire. You only have to believe. On several occasions Jesus had to rebuke His disciples by saying, "Ye of little faith, why do you doubt?" Renounce to unbelief today, and accept God's blessings.

Prosperity is For You

God's prosperity is within your reach. Financial ruin remains represented by thorns and thistles, and by the crown of thorns Jesus bore on His brow, He removed the curse of ruin from us. He made Himself poor so that we might be made rich, and this is what His Word teaches.

Prosperity is not something reserved for just a few. No! Prosperity is something God reserves for each one of His children.

Every battle you have endured until now has represented steps to get you closer to Him. The lack of resources, the hard times at home, the situation at work, the condition of your country, etc., have only been steps to bring you closer to Him. In fact, you already are a child of God, and God's children are prosperous. King David teaches: "I have been young, and now am old, yet I have not seen the righteous forsaken nor his descendants begging bread" (Psalm 37:25). Paul remarked: "And my God shall supply all your need according to His riches in glory by Christ Jesus" (Philippians 4:19). These are fundamental principles. If a river of prosperity surges towards you, what would you do? Will you say, "I don't deserve it," and move aside? Of course not! Stand at the foot of the Cross, and ask the Lord to pour that river of prosperity over you.

The Lord spoke through the prophet Haggai: "The silver is Mine, and the gold is Mine . . ." (Haggai 2:8). Your Father is owner of all the silver and gold, so tell Him: "Lord Jesus, You are God's prosperity and I want You to fill me and saturate my life with Your prosperity. I want prosperity to be in my life." If prosperity was not reserved for all of God's children, He would simply say not to ask because it is only for Jews. But prosperity belongs to everyone who has Jesus in their heart. You should not be afraid to ask for it. Do not think you are somehow less spiritual when you pray for prosperity.

We must pray for souls to come to Jesus and we must also pray for the Lord to bless our finances. Agur said: "Two things I ask of you, O LORD; do not refuse me before I die: Keep falsehood and lies far from me; give me neither poverty nor riches, but give me only my daily bread. Otherwise, I may have too much and disown you and say, 'Who is the LORD ?' Or I may become poor and steal, and so dishonor the name of my God" (Proverbs 30:7-9).

Why is it that God does not prosper many? It is because prosperity may destroy them. Some are not emotionally fit to administer prosperity. They either do not know how to manage their possessions, or they get money and spend it wrongly. We know that prosperity in the hands of fools will destroy them. The curse of ruin comes to some as a result of the wrong use of their money. It is not that God has withheld the money. Ruin comes from their improper handling of money. "Our fathers sinned and are no more, but we bear their iniquities" (Lamentations 5:7). These days, God is differentiating between righteous and unrighteous. He is prospering the righteous while the unrighteous live through all kinds of difficulties. I know that little in the hands of the righteous avails much, but the unrighteous does not know what to do because he does not know where to go. The righteous knows that he can run to God who will prosper him.

PRINCIPLES TO HELP YOU ENTER INTO PROSPERITY

1. You Must Receive the Spirit or Breath of God

"And the LORD God formed man of the dust of the ground, and breathed into his nostrils the breath of life; and man became a living being" (Genesis 2:7). The word "breath" in the original Hebrew is "Ruah." It is a guttural, sustained breath that comes from the deepest part of God who breathes it on man to provide him with life. Man received this breath which is the very Spirit of God. Job said: "As long as the breath (Ruah) of God is within me, my lips will not speak wickedness" (Job 27:3-4). What makes us different from other creatures is God's breath. You are intelligent and different from others; you are made in the image of Jesus Christ by the breath of God. He who does not have the "ruah" of God, cannot live the Christian life; he is different from those who have Jesus in their heart. A person who does not have Jesus, though very prosperous, will have riches that will not last, since he will spend eternity separated from God. Let us remember that the word "death" means separation, and those who are eternally separated from God will suffer eternal torment. When God created us, He breathed "ruah" on us—His breath. Because of man's sin, "ruah" departed, but when man comes back to Christ, the "ruah" returns. For this reason, Jesus, before He was taken up to heaven breathed on His disciples and established "ruah" over the government of the twelve saying: "...Receive the Holy Spirit" (John 20:22). At that moment, God's "ruah" returned to us. Therefore, in order to enter into prosperity, you must have the breath, the Spirit of God.

2. God Has Already Planted a Garden for You

"The LORD God planted a garden eastward in Eden, and there He put the man whom He had formed. And out of the ground the LORD God made every tree grow that is pleasant to the sight and good for food. The tree of life was also in the midst of the garden and the tree of the knowledge of good and evil" (Genesis 2:8-9). The Scriptures tell us in the book of Genesis that God planted a garden in Eden. Notice that Adam did not cultivate or plant the garden; he only enjoyed it. In the same way, God has planted a garden of blessings for you. You do not have to work for them. Many have established a pattern in their minds and have become accustomed to walking through life according to that pattern so that they cannot see God's blessings.

For this reason, they die filled with complaints, bitterness and pain, thinking that God forgot them, did not care for them, nor provide for their needs. All of this is because they could not see the riches He had for them, and because they would not break the pattern.

One of the couples who worked as pastors with us in Bogotá was settling into their new home, and they invited us to come and see it. When we arrived, we realized that neither the apartment nor the neighborhood were appropriate for them to live in. They were enjoying a new home, however, we encouraged them to think big and conquer something even better. For them, this was a great challenge. Three years later, they were settled in one of the best neighborhoods of Bogotá. They had been living in their new home for two months when I was ministering to them during a meeting. The Spirit gave me a word for them: "Children, if I want to bless you, why do you weep? Why do you refuse my blessing and feel unworthy of it?" When they heard this word, they began to cry and ask the Lord for forgiveness. Since moving into their new home and seeing how beautiful and glamorous everything was, they had felt unworthy. They had felt guilty for enjoying such blessings when there were so many who were suffering.

Do not make the same mistake. If God wants to bless you, do not refuse His blessings. Do not complain or whine, just give praise to God.

3. God Planted a Tree of Blessing for You

"And out of the ground the LORD God made every tree grow that is pleasant to the sight and good for food. The tree of life was also in the midst of the garden and the tree of the knowledge of good and evil" (Genesis 2:9). This passage describes the tree as "pleasant to the sight," and this is a type of all the blessings that God has for your life. "Every good gift and every perfect gift is from above, and comes down from the Father of lights, with whom there is no variation or shadow of turning" (James 1:17). When the Apostle refers to "every good gift," he means all prosperity, all excellence, and everything you may grow in this life; it all comes from the Father of lights.

It is God's desire to always bless, but many reject His blessings because they have been taught that they must live in poverty. They base this teaching on the passage that says, "blessed are the poor in spirit..." (Matthew 5:3). Matthew says: "Blessed are the poor in spirit...," not those who do not have money to pay their rent, because that does not carry a blessing. The good gift comes from the Father of lights, the One who has enough for you so that you can bless others.

The Lord taught that He would make us the head and not the tail, that we would lend to many nations and not borrow (see Deuteronomy 28:12-13).

"The blessing of the LORD makes one rich, and He adds no sorrow with it" (Proverbs 10:22). God's blessings enrich and He gives you the privilege of enjoying it. God will not prosper your finances and allow your child to have an infirmity. He will not prosper your finances and allow your family to be destroyed. God's blessing is complete, that is, He will bless your finances, your family, your health and your ministry.

4. The Tree is Pleasant to the Sight

"And out of the ground the LORD God made every tree grow that is pleasant to the sight and good for food. The tree of life was also in the midst of the garden and the tree of the knowledge of good and evil" (Genesis 2:9). The tree was pleasant to the eyes. This means that you have to see with your spiritual eyes the pleasant blessings that God has prepared in advance. The first couple God created were not slaves to lust, lasciviousness, adultery, fornication, etc. They were spiritual beings. You are a spiritual being living in a body of flesh. Adam had received God's breath; he had God's nature. God had told him to see the blessings, which was the tree of blessing. There were two trees: one which contained all of the blessings, and the other which would draw them away from God's purpose. Regrettably, Eve did not want to go to the tree that contained God's blessing. She went to the other tree and looked upon it. Satan seized the moment and said: "For God knows that in the day you eat of it your eyes will be opened, and you will be like God, knowing good and evil" (Genesis 3:5). Eve saw that the tree was good to eat and she exchanged what was "good" for what was "appealing." There are things that appear to be good to the eyes but actually lead to destruction.

The apostle Paul said: "But as it is written: 'Eye has not seen, nor ear heard, nor have entered into the heart of man the things which God has prepared for those who love Him.' But God has revealed them to us through His Spirit. For the Spirit searches all things, yes, the deep things of God" (1 Corinthians 2:9-10).

The things that the "eye has not seen" are those of the tree of blessing that God planted for man; things that Adam and Eve did not see in the Garden of Eden because they were focusing on the tree that offered them human wisdom, exalted their ego, and exalted them. But the apostle Paul says that when we turn to Jesus, that tree is restored to us, and our spiritual eyes are opened to see all the blessings of God. Everything, however, happens through Jesus. It is only when one enters into intimacy with Him that the spiritual eyes are opened and one begins to see the miracles.

God's blessing means that a man can have a family, people with whom to share, the ability to provide for his family, and enjoy good health. You must begin to see the blessings in faith. Note that blessings do not come from hard work, but rather, by looking at the tree. When you enter into intimacy with God, He gives you a word that bears fruit in your heart (it is a promise that becomes real to your life). For example, when you take the promise that says, "And my God shall supply all your need according to His riches in glory by Christ Jesus" (Philippians 4:19), confess that word and believe that God will prosper and bless you. At that moment, all of your needs will be supplied because you will have already conquered them through faith.

5. The Tree Was Good to Eat

God always wants the best for us and in order to prove that something is good, you must taste it. The ear tests the words, taste buds tests the food, but you will never know what the blessings of God are until you taste them. How can you taste the blessings of God? Tithing is an example. The Lord said:

"Bring all the tithes into the storehouse, that there may be food in My house, and try Me now in this, Says the LORD of hosts, If I will not open for you the windows of heaven and pour out for you the windows of heaven and pour out for you such blessing that there will not be room enough to receive it" (Malachi 3:10). Just as I have tasted the blessing of tithing, I have tasted the curse of unfaithfulness. The greatest crisis I have lived through in my life came as a result of committing a sum of money to a business instead of the church.

That same day, all financial blessing stopped. I was not able to prosper in spite of my praying, fasting and spiritual warfare. Until God revealed that all this economic oppression had been upon me because of my unfaithfulness in tithing, and if I did not repent and make restitution, He would not be able to bless me (I will talk more about this later on). God does not need our money, but He will test our faithfulness and commitment to Him by how we administer it.

6. God Wants to Give You the Tree of Life

"For whoever finds me finds life, and obtains favor from the LORD" (Proverbs 8:35). The tree of life represents Jesus of Nazareth. This is why Jesus says that whoever finds Him finds life. Job went through many financial trials where he lost everything. The book of Job says that it was fear that led him to that situation. But when his trust was renewed once again in God, he had an encounter with the tree of life, repented, humbled himself, cried out for mercy, and God restored him.

The door to enter into intimacy with God is repentance. If you want to step through that door, you must leave behind your past, for it is impossible to enter with a sinful life. You must turn to God with all of your heart, your mind and your soul. You must dare to trust in Him, renouncing everything you have been and done, and connect with the tree of life. When you step through the door of repentance into a life of faith, you will find that God's blessings have already been prepared for you.

Paul said: "Blessed be the God and Father of our Lord Jesus Christ, who has blessed us with every spiritual blessing in the heavenly places in Christ" (Ephesians 1:3). When you are reconciled with God, all of His blessings, the tree of life, and all of the delicious fruit which is good to eat, will come to your life.

Every one of God's blessings are reserved in the spirit, and when you live in the spirit, the blessings become a reality. This will take place as you learn to bring everything you need from the spiritual to the natural realm through prayer, confession of the Word, and visualization. When you move in the dimension of faith, God guides you to where you need to be, where you need to work, what actions to take, and what business ventures to undertake—seeing the blessings in everything you do.

PROSPERITY IS COMPLETE

God's purpose is to prosper His children, not only spiritually, but also physically and materially. Just as the apostle John tells the elder Gaius: "Beloved, I pray that you may prosper in all things and be in health, just as your soul prospers" (3 John 2). Many times the believer thinks that an adverse situation, like a financial crisis, has been pre-established by God, and that through various difficulties we are brought closer to Him. Throughout the whole biblical framework, we find that when the Lord sent His disciples, He instructed them not to take any provisions because they would find them along the way. The second time He sent them, He instructed them to take all kinds of provisions so that they would have no need. There are times when we completely depend on God and we lack nothing. While there are other times when we make our own provision and we lack nothing.

Trust in the Right Source

As I mentioned before, years ago I went through a very difficult financial situation, and I was behind in various commitments. In the midst of my need, I sought help from my family and friends. I did not have anyone else to turn to.

I made an effort to work harder. I would awake early in the day and come home late at night, tired and without results. I could not understand what was happening since I have always tried to live in obedience to the Word. I would think: "This can't be happening. If I'm a Christian, God has to provide for all my needs. What kind of a witness am I going to be? If I am to preach about abundance, I must live in abundance." This caused me to seek God earnestly in prayer. I told Him: "God, I need an answer to my need and You have the answer." While in prayer, God answered me. He reminded me how eight months prior–when my business was successful–I received my pay, listened to a friend's advice, and invested it in another business venture, including the tithe that belonged to the Lord. I thought I saw it so simple. In just fifteen days, I would have recovered the money invested and much more (I thought the tithe would also be greater).

The fact is, I never saw the money again. It disappeared in an instant. I missed out on the blessing, because all these things take place in the spiritual kingdom. When a person gives their tithe and offering, it has spiritual repercussions. God activates His angels and causes that seed the person is giving, to multiply and bear fruit. When they are not faithful in tithing, the angels are tied up and cannot work. The devourer, who is in charge of robbing finances, is then active in the situation. He has many ways to steal money: through alcoholism in a family member, an accident, or a sudden illness where you end up having to invest great sums of money to cover the costs. When you fail to give your tithes to the Lord, you open a door to the enemy and the devourer comes to steal your finances.

The Tithes Belong Only to the Lord

The Lord helped me see that I had done wrong. I understood that I could not do with His money as I pleased. Do you pay your taxes? Imagine for a moment, that you are due to pay your taxes and you have the money; however, a business opportunity suddenly comes up and you invest the money and default on your taxes. Will the government put up with it? Of course not! If you do not pay your taxes, it is the same as stealing from the government. Many do not understand that the same principle applies to tithing. When you do not bring your tithe to the Lord, you invite ruin into your life.

Some may see a family in need, and reason: "This is tax money. The government has plenty of money and I don't even know what they do with it. Yet this family is in real need so I am going to help them by giving them my tax money. When I file my taxes, I will tell them that I did a good deed." Will this be a valid argument? There are many people who act the same way with the Lord's money. They say, "Well, since there are so many people in need, I'd rather do a good deed and help the poor and needy." You may be generous with your own money, but not with the Lord's. The purpose of the tithe is to increase the work of God.

Notice the question God asks: "Will a man rob God? Yet you rob me. But you ask, 'How do we rob you?' In tithes and offerings. You are under a curse—the whole nation of you— because you are robbing me" (Malachi 3:8-9, NIV). When you use your tithe inappropriately, it brings the judgment of a curse, because that money has been contaminated by the sin of stealing. This will cause the forces of evil to strategically attack your life and your family.

-"Bring all the tithes into the storehouse" (Commandment). What is the storehouse? It is the Church, because it carries out the administration to insure that there will be food in the whole house of the Lord.

- "'And try me now in this', says the LORD of hosts, 'If I will not open for you the windows of heaven and pour out for you such blessing that there will be not room enough to receive it'" (Malachi 3:10).

I do not know of any religious or secular organization that can grow without finances. God could have sent angels to directly supply for His work, but He always uses man. And for that reason, to redeem mankind, God had to become man, and being found as a man, gave His life for us. In the same way, in order to make His Church prosper, God uses man, who in this case are believers. If there is an area where God shows Himself to be jealous, it is in regard to His work. This is the reason why He presents a challenge to them, to tithe faithfully and to test Him in this to see: "If I will not open for you the windows of heaven and pour out for you such blessing that there will not be room enough to receive it" (Malachi 3:10).

When the Lord allowed me to see that I had failed Him with my tithes, I said a prayer of confession. Confession comes after repentance. In order to receive mercy, one must repent from his sin, confess it and renounce it. Later on, God led me to enter into a covenant with Him, and I committed myself in the following three areas:

The Provision of God for Your Life

1. Faithfulness in Giving Ten Percent

I committed to be faithful with my tithe and to give an additional ten percent for a total of twenty percent. There are companies that started tithing fifteen percent, and then they increased to twenty, then thirty, until some are giving ninety percent and living only on ten percent. You can imagine how much this company makes! There is great prosperity when you are faithful to the Lord. "...for it is He who gives you power to get wealth, that He may establish His covenant which He swore to your fathers, as it is this day" (Deuteronomy 8:18).

2. Acknowledge Him as the Only Source of My Provision

I told Him: "For all You have given me; I will never give glory to my intellect, skills or abilities. All the glory will be only and exclusively Yours." You should not seek to have possessions in order to boast or to be filled with pride, because it is not healthy and can lead to losing God's blessing. Seek to have possessions to enhance the work of God.

3. To Be a Good Steward of That Which He Has Given Me

I prayed saying: "You will be the owner of everything I receive. Whenever You ask for something, I will supply it, because everything belongs to You." When I rose from my knees, in my spirit, I already felt like a prosperous man. The next day, I had an appointment with a beloved servant of God. As we were talking, he looked at me and said: "Have you been having financial difficulties?" "That's correct," I responded, and proceeded to tell him about my situation. At once he pulled out his checkbook and gave me a substantial love offering with which I was able to pay some of my obligations. When I received the check, I was so excited that I did not know whether to cash it or frame it. Since then, I have been walking on the path of prosperity.

God's provision is abundant, because He is a God of abundance, and He wants to reveal it to His people so that each one of His children may enter into the dimension of prosperity. "But as it is written: 'Eye has not seen, nor ear heard, nor have entered into the heart of man the things which God has prepared for those who love Him.'" But God has revealed them to us through His Spirit. For the Spirit searches all things, yes, the deep things of God. For what man knows the things of a man except the spirit of the man which is in him? Even so no one knows the things of God except the Spirit of God. Now we have received, not the spirit of the world, but the Spirit who is from God, that we might know the things that have been freely given to us by God. These things we also speak, not in words which man's wisdom teaches but which the Holy Spirit teaches, comparing spiritual things with spiritual. But the natural man does not receive the things of the Spirit of God, for they are foolishness to him; nor can he know them, because they are spiritually discerned. But he who is spiritual judges all things, yet he himself is rightly judged by no one. "'For who has known the mind of the LORD that he may instruct him?' But we have the mind of Christ" (1 Corinthians 2:16).

God has prepared a blessing for each of His children that goes beyond the natural. Even though it has not reached sight or ear or thoughts, it is found in God's heart. You can walk in prosperity, because if you can believe God and His Word, you are prosperous and have entered into the dimension of prosperity. Solomon said: "The blessing of the LORD makes one rich, and He adds no sorrow with it" (Proverbs 10:22).

The apostle James taught: "You do not have because you do not ask. You ask and do not receive, because you ask amiss, that you may spend it on your pleasures" (James 4:2-3).

Something I have learned is that God has much more to give us than we can ask for. For that reason, we must be specific in our prayers and should not be afraid to ask. My wife and I usually make a list of our different needs. We present them to the Lord, believing that He always responds to each of the requests we make.

We can testify that every single request we have made of the Lord has been answered. God is pleased when we come to Him in humility, and tell Him we need His help.

"Lord, forgive me because for a long time I thought that Your provision for me was very limited and that I could not go beyond the portion You had allotted me. Now my eyes are open and I can see that the blessings You have prepared for me are limitless. My heart has been illuminated by a ray of hope. I know that what You have to give me goes beyond what I could ever ask because all my needs were already conquered and supplied on the Cross. I come today, in genuine faith, nearer to that tree of blessing to partake of the fruit that grants me prosperity. I know that anything I might desire I will obtain because You, Lord, will supply all my needs according to Your riches in glory. Lord, I pray that You will renew my mind so that I can stay in this spirit of conquest and that I may also help others. In Jesus' name, Amen."

Chapter 7

FORGIVENESS IS THE FOUNDATION OF REDEMPTION

"And forgive us our debts, as we forgive our debtors. And do not lead us into temptation, but deliver us from the evil one. For Thine is the kingdom and the power and the glory forever, amen. For if you forgive men their trespasses, your heavenly Father will also forgive you. But if you do not forgive men their trespasses, neither will your Father forgive your trespasses."

(Matthew 6:12-15)

The Lord taught in the book of John that God so loved the world that He gave His only begotten Son, that whosoever believes in Him should not perish, but have eternal life (see John 3:16).

We were all completely separated from God, destined for eternal condemnation. Our rebellion separated us from God, but His mercy was great and He did not want to take into account the sins of men and instead established a way to redeem and extend His forgiveness. We all need this forgiveness and we can receive it, but we can also give it.

In the Lord's Prayer, the only commentary that Jesus made was in relation to sin, when He said: "For if you forgive men their trespasses, your heavenly Father will also forgive you. But if you do not forgive men their trespasses, neither will your Father forgive your trespasses" (Matthew 6:14-15).

The best medicine for the human being is forgiveness. Forgiveness breaks the strongest chains. Forgiveness opens the most secure doors. Forgiveness knocks down the thickest walls. Nothing compares to this forgiveness, and the best way to show forgiveness is through the Cross.

Forgiveness of God

If you look at the Cross of Christ you will note that there are two beams: one vertical and the other horizontal.

The vertical beam speaks of the forgiveness that God gives to man. Jesus died with open arms saying to humanity that His arms were open wide in offering forgiveness. The horizontal beam speaks of the forgiveness that man can give to one another. But who do we have to forgive? Everyone who has offended us. Those who have caused most harm in a person's heart are those closest to him. Surely you are not upset with a businessman in a commercial establishment or with the manager of some company, but rather, with those who live under your own roof. Those are the people whom you must forgive.

Some may close their hearts and say they cannot forgive someone who hurt them deeply, and they choose to continue punishing them with a whip of indifference. This does not make others suffer because the one who is hurt is the person who has the resentment. When someone offers forgiveness, the first person set free is the one who grants forgiveness first. Before forgiveness reaches others, it first touches the forgiver's life, and breaks the chains of resentment.

Forgiveness brings reconciliation, harmony and fellowship. But closing the heart with unforgiveness leads to bitterness, discord, hatefulness and war. The Psalmist said: "Blessed is he whose transgression is forgiven, whose sin is covered" (Psalm 32:1). There is a special blessing when forgiveness takes place. When we receive forgiveness from God, He breaks our chains, and brings true happiness and joy into our lives. That is why the Psalmist says that happy and joyful is the man who has received forgiveness from God. When God forgives, it is easy to receive, but it is difficult to give it to others.

Forgiving Debt

In the parable of the two debtors (see Matthew 18:23-25), the Lord Jesus speaks of a king who asks a man to pay his debt. Because he did not have the money, he asked for more time. The debt this man had, translated into today's money, would be approximately six million dollars; an impossible debt to pay. For this reason, the king listened to his request and decided to forgive the debt. But later, the same man who had received the pardon, encountered another man who owed him a small debt, and he asked him to pay it. When that man said he did not have the money and asked for time to pay it, he became enraged and sent him to jail. This fact got back to the king, who had forgiven him of such a great debt, and he sent for him. He asked why he had not forgiven the debt like his had been forgiven, and how much the debt was. Translated into today's money, it would be sixteen dollars. The king became angry and asked him: "If I forgave you of such a great debt, why couldn't you pardon such a small one? With that attitude, your debt is reinstated." The landlord sent him to jail and turned him over to be tortured until his entire debt was paid.

Many people go to church to ask forgiveness from God, but later they cannot forgive their spouse. They do not understand that the Lord forgives our offenses in the measure that we forgive those indebted to us. That is to say, the forgiveness that you give to another is the same forgiveness that you will receive. The Lord measures with the same measure that we use. When one resists forgiving, all his transgressions come back to his life. To forgive is to forget, because that is what Jesus did with our sins. When God forgives, He forgets completely. The book of Psalms declares that, as far as the east is from the west, that is how far our sins and our rebellions are from Him, and He will remember them no more. When you forgive, do it with faith and without fear that you will be sinned against again, and believe that the person has received your forgiveness.

Counsel from the Lord for receiving and giving forgiveness:

1. Recognize Your Need to Forgive

Nobody can say they do not need God's forgiveness. We are all sinners and have rebelled against Him, and if you need God to forgive you, you must also give forgiveness. The first words of the Lord Jesus on the Cross were, "Father, forgive them, for they do not know what they do" (Luke 23:34a).

After we were victims of the assassins, it was very difficult for me to maintain the same enthusiasm in my prayer life; I did not feel peaceful. I said to the Lord in prayer: "God, help me. I want to feel like I did before. Make me free of all uncertainty." At that moment, I heard the voice of the Lord say: "Have you forgiven those that tried to kill you?" Before that word, my prayer had been, "God, give my enemy justice." I wanted God to render His judgment on those people, but the Lord asked me, "Can you forgive them?" I said, "Lord, today I forgive those people that wanted to take my life. I forgive the planners and executors, and I bless them in the name of Jesus. Let what they did to us be the means that You use so they come to know You." Immediately after I said that prayer, I felt the power of God come into my life, and His presence anew. Later, the Lord told me: "The entire time resentment is in a person's heart, they will be stuck in the past." It is like there has been a pause in their life, but when true forgiveness is extended, the pause is lifted.

2. You Must Submit Yourself to God

When someone submits to God, they can resist bitterness and resentment. "Therefore submit to God. Resist the devil and he will flee from you. Draw near to God and He will draw near to you. Cleanse your hands, you sinners; and purify your hearts, you double-minded" (James 4:7-8). You cannot overcome the adversary if you do not submit completely to God. This implies living a life of obedience to His Word. God happily shepherds those who have teachable and humble hearts before Him. There was a time when a couple came to see me and wanted to talk with me. The wife was in a lot of pain because she had found out that her husband had been unfaithful several years before. She was resentful towards God, because in the depth of her heart, she blamed Him for having failed her by not stopping the infidelity of her spouse.

Her spiritual life was drying up because of this bitterness. She even started to think she would never be able to be useful in ministry again. When I told her that God wanted to bless her in His service, her face lit up and a light of hope came into her life. But I warned her that it was necessary to forgive her spouse with all her heart to make this a reality. She answered me, "I can't trust him. Can you guarantee that he's not going to fail me again?" I explained to her that forgiveness is an act of faith, just as one day God believed in us and forgave us with all His heart, forgetting about all the bad that we had done. God forgives and forgets. Later I asked her, "Maybe God needs to forgive you of something?" She answered, "Yes, a lot." That day, that woman made the decision to forgive her husband with all her heart. In her own words, she said: "I will never let another negative thought into my mind towards you." When she finished praying, they hugged, cried, and a complete restoration came into their lives.

This woman submitted her life to God, and in spite of the fact that the enemy had worked in her thoughts for many years, she was able to extend genuine forgiveness. With this act of faith, the adversary lost complete control of her life and she was able to resist doubt and fear in the name of Jesus.

Throughout the years of my Christian life, I have learned to live daily in genuine submission to God, achieving it through forgiveness. By taking each offense to the Cross of Calvary and by the blood of Jesus, I have transformed pain into strength, and have been able to resist the adversary and tear down every argument that he has raised up against us (see 2 Corinthians 10:4-5).

3. Forgiveness Delivers Us from Guilt

Many people say they do not have the desire to forgive and that is because forgiveness is not a feeling, but a decision of the heart. We do not forgive people because they deserve it, but because it is the character of Christ. If we can forgive small sins, we will be prepared to forgive those which seem larger to us. He who is faithful in forgiving the small things will also forgive big things.

Pastor Cho speaks of a woman who was a victim of guilt. Although she had a beautiful home and enjoyed all types of comforts, she felt like the most impure woman in the world, because of a secret relationship she had had with her brother-in-law. She felt like there was no forgiveness. But Pastor Cho told her: "Try to imagine a big lake, and that someone comes up and throws in a little rock. When it hits the water, the sound it produces is a "plop." Later, you take a much larger stone and throw it in the water. The sound is similar to the first one, but much stronger. Both stones go to the same place. The sins of some people are small, and they have to go to the depths of the ocean. The sins of others are great and they also have to go to the same place." When she understood this, she was able to, in an act of faith, release herself of all the weight she had carried. She felt that all her sins were forgiven by

Jesus, and she received complete freedom. From that time on, she was able to live a full and blessed life.

4. Confess That You Have Been Forgiven

Sometimes it is not necessary to confess forgiveness to the other person because the forgiveness is unilateral. In that case, one must pray naming the person, even though they are not present, forgiving and blessing them. It is possible that when you make that decision, the enemy will speak to your mind or you will receive thoughts about that person which seem to revive the thoughts you have just decided to renounce. You simply must not accept them, because you have already decided to forgive.

Once you forgive, it is not necessary to forgive again, just confess that you have done it, and give thanks to God for it. It is like canceling a debt and tearing up the note. It is not necessary to tear it up again. The offense is the debt, and the forgiveness is the cancellation.

5. You Cannot Return to Resentment

You cannot let the enemy fill your mind and heart with arguments again. You must completely forget what has happened. Avoid insinuation and hurtful thoughts. The forgiveness must be complete. Never give life to resentment once it has been buried. I have known of several cases where a person refused to forgive their spouse and the result was the destruction of the whole family. Resentment makes everybody lose; it becomes a wall of separation that damages the family. We know that a house divided against itself cannot stand. On the other hand, the person that forgives from the heart benefits himself, but he is also practicing true love, just like Jesus. His first words on the Cross were: "Father, forgive them because they do not know what they are doing." Jesus repeated those words continually, and this helped Him to complete His task.

I remember a case of a woman who had a beautiful home and the perfect husband, who was responsible and very affectionate with his children. She trusted him completely because she had never seen any odd behavior from him. Then one day, everything they had built together over many years, collapsed. It all started because of a thought that entered into her mind. She went to the bank one day and they asked her the following question: "Which account do you want to deposit into?" She was surprised because she did not know he had more than one bank account. As the days passed, she discovered that that was not all. Her husband had another woman, with whom he had a daughter. This person had worked with them years before. In the midst of her pain, she clung to a promise given by God in His Word: "Therefore whoever hears these sayings of Mine, and does them, I will liken him to a wise man who built his house on the rock" (Matthew 7:24).

She decided to confront her husband and give him the opportunity to leave the other woman or decide to stay with her. Her husband cried bitterly, repenting, begging forgiveness, and at the same time promised he would be forever faithful.

The wife was filled with courage and confronted the other woman saying: "I forgive you for the damage you have done to our home, but I am absolutely certain you cannot destroy it because it is built on the Rock." She forgave her, blessed her, and took her to a Christian church. She said that even though her husband had a daughter outside of marriage, she would never allow doubt or negativity, but always live clinging to the promise.

Today, her husband is a great blessing and they enjoy a beautiful family together.

Avoid bitter words and insinuation, and do not permit resentment to return to your life. Paul said: "For if I build again those things which I destroyed, I make myself a transgressor" (Galatians 2:18).

6. Displace the Negative With the Positive
The Bible says that he who is forgiven much, the same loves much. When someone believes that God has forgiven a little, he is going to love a little. But when one knows that God has forgiven a mountain of sins, he is going to love with all his heart. If the sins of the one you forgive were great, decide to believe in that person with all your heart and never remember their sins. Bury those transgressions and see how God gives you restoration.

During the rule of Andrew Jackson–one of the Presidents of the United States–a man in the U.S. Postal Service named George Wilson, realized that somebody was stealing from him. When he saw the thief, he took his gun, shot and killed him. He was condemned to death for that act. When he found out about it, President Jackson extended a pardon, but George Wilson would not accept it. A great legal debate arose and the case went to the Supreme Court. The court gave an opinion that said: "The declaration of pardon is only a piece of paper but it has the power to pardon if the person being pardoned accepts it. If the person being pardoned declines to accept it, the sentence cannot be set aside. The death sentence must be carried out against George Wilson." George Wilson was executed for refusing to accept the pardon that had been granted unto him.

God extends His pardon, but we determine whether we accept it or reject it. He that accepts it receives all the benefits of the Cross in his life. The one that rejects it receives the curse described by God in His Word. A great difference exists between those who attend church, live as if God never forgave their sins, think the Word of God is worthless, treat God like a liar, and those who have faith and dare to trust Him because their sins are forgiven.

"Lord, I know that You are the greatest example of forgiveness that has ever existed. You forgave all my faults. You erased my sin and forgot them. Thank you, Jesus. Today, I ask You to put that same love in my heart to be willing to forgive those who have harmed me. Fill me of You, God, with Your love and forgiveness. In Your name, I ask, Amen."

Chapter 8

OVERCOMING TEMPTATION THROUGH FAITH

"And do not lead us into temptation..."
(Matthew 6:13)

The meaning of "do not lead us into temptation" is, "give us the strength or the faith to stand up to it." People fall into temptation for lack of faith when they take their eyes off Jesus and they sink.

Something similar happened with Peter when he had an encounter with Jesus walking on the water (see Matthew 14:27-33). He looked at the circumstances, began to sink, and shouted: "Lord, help me. I'm drowning!" Jesus extended His hand and said to him: "Why did you doubt, man of little faith?" What made Peter sink was a lack of faith. Someone with a high level of faith will never fall, so we must stay strong in our faith.

Overcoming Temptation

We all face temptation of one kind or another, and the only way to overcome it is by having faith. Remember, we are in a human body, but we are spiritual beings. Your nature is spiritual, so your spirit must dominate the physical. The people of Israel did not understand this principle. They tried to live in the flesh and wanted to make the spiritual nature similar to the physical nature. They did not understand how to live by faith, because of this, God was displeased and they died in the wilderness. The Apostle says: "The people sat down to eat and drink and got up to indulge in pagan revelry" (1 Corinthians 10:7, NIV). The people were unrestrained in their sin and because all unrestrained sin leads to idolatry, they were ultimately destroyed. This is why the apostle Paul warns about idolatry and fornication.

Maintaining Holiness

When God created us, He considered our sexuality, which is to be pure and holy within marriage, but outside of marriage, it is fornication and adultery. The book of Joshua tells what the people of Israel had to conquer. God had given them the land of Canaan, but the Moabites, who wanted to conquer the Israelites, asked advice from a false prophet named Balaam, who told them that to be successful, the Moabite women should have sex with the Israelite men. They then began to mix together. The people of Israel broke the covenant, and this provoked God's wrath, and in one day, more then twenty-three thousand people died.

Our body is the temple of the Holy Spirit. When the body is given to fornication, it is a sin that is committed directly against the temple of God, which is a profaning of the sacred and triggers the wrath of God.

Paul said: "Do you not know that the wicked will not inherit the kingdom of God? Do not be deceived; neither the sexually immoral nor idolaters nor male prostitutes nor homosexual offenders…" (1 Corinthians 6:9).

Guarding Our Speech

The other warning that the apostle gives, is that we should not murmur. Murmuring is always a sin committed with the tongue. Murmuring is to complain and speak badly about a situation, whether it is about your finances, your life, your leaders, those in political powers, or about the country where you live. All murmuring is of the devil, and because of that, it brings the judgment of God on the people. Everyone who gives voice to murmuring is simply opening the door to the destroyer and all that the destroyer, touches will come to an end. Jesus also said not to tempt the Lord nor put Him to the test or challenge Him. The Lord said: "Do not tempt the LORD your God." The people of Israel had these experiences because they were living according to their carnal nature. They wanted to serve a spiritual God with a carnal mind, and that is impossible. You can not fake Christianity. The Christian life is Christ living through you. That is why when you have the character of Christ you can live in the dimension of faith.

You Must Know the Reality of the Spiritual World

You must know that just as God exists, so does the adversary. There are opposite poles in this world. There is light and darkness, justice and injustice, good and evil, hot and cold. You must understand that you are on one of two sides; you cannot be on both sides at the same time. You cannot have one foot with God and the other with the devil; one foot in the darkness and one in the light. You have to make a decision to serve Jesus and stand by His side. Paul said that we were transferred from the power of Satan to the power of Christ. Before then, we were children of wrath; we belonged to the kingdom of darkness because we were ignorant. But now we are children of the light, and we belong to the kingdom of Jesus Christ, because He gave us life and life abundantly.

You Must Strengthen Yourself in the Lord

Finally, be strong in the Lord and in His mighty power, says the Word (see Ephesians 6:10). The Apostle invites us to keep our confidence high. David, in one of the psalms, said: "He restores my soul" (Psalm 23:3). This means that when we are intimate with God, He fills us with His presence, breathing the breath of life within us, and through prayer, we can see circumstances changed for the positive. No matter what battles we are fighting, as we come to the Lord with our burdens in times of intimacy, in the secret place, something happens. We feel the balm of His Spirit covering our whole being, and at the same time we can think about the Cross and feel crucified with the Lord Jesus Christ. When this happens, our weakness becomes our strength. We are filled with inner strength that we did not have before, and our whole being is energized, ready to stand up and conquer.

Use the Armor of God Daily

"Put on the full armor of God so that you can take your stand against the devil's schemes" (Ephesians 6:11).

We must put on the whole armor of God to be strong against the devil's schemes. Why would God prepare armor for each one of us? Because we do not fight against flesh and blood, but against principalities, against powers, against the rulers of darkness of this age, and against the spiritual forces of evil in the heavenly places. The battle was not declared against people, but against the demonic powers of evil. Paul said that we take on the armor of God so we can stand firm in the evil day. The evil day is the day of adversity. It is the day of testing.

As a family, we lived that "evil day" when our assassination was attempted. It was as if the protection of God had been broken, and that God had allowed the devil to enter and do as he pleased in our lives. We experienced the terror of hell.

It never crossed my mind, that as a family, we would go through something like that. I received five bullets in my body, while my wife received one. Our daughters were horrified by what they were seeing. During the ten days that I was in the hospital, none of the doctors thought they would be able to save me. But thanks to the faith of my wife, my daughters, my family and church, we survived that bitter cup–obtaining victory in the evil day. After the test, the restoration was quick, the healing in the hearts of my daughters was instantaneous, and it contributed to our family relationships becoming much stronger.

The very Sunday we were attacked, I had preached on the topic, "The Power of Blessing," and we as a church had prayed the Lord's Prayer. We all put on the armor of God by faith, and within ten minutes of leaving that meeting, we were attacked. Months later I asked the Lord, "Why didn't You protect us that Sunday, if we had on the armor of God?" His answer surprised me: "Son, if I had not protected you, you would not be alive today in this body. The shot you took in the head did not go straight in, but grazed your skull because you had on the helmet of salvation to protect your head. The bullet that went into your neck did not destroy a single organ because you had on the steel mesh that warriors of antiquity used. The two shots that hit you in the chest did not hurt you because you had on the breastplate of righteousness. Even the shot to your heart (which was deviated by your watch) was turned aside because you wore the steel bracelet those warriors wore. Son, thanks to the fact that you had put on the armor your life was spared."

THE WEAPONS OF BATTLE

"Put on the whole armor of God that you may be able to stand against the wiles of the devil, for we do not wrestle against flesh and blood, but against principalities, against powers, against the rulers of the darkness of this age, against the spiritual hosts of wickedness in the heavenly places. Therefore, take up the whole armor of God that you may be able to withstand in the evil day, and having done all, to stand. Stand, therefore, having girded your waist with truth, having put on the breastplate of righteousness, and having shod your feet with the preparation of the gospel of peace, above all, taking the shield of faith, with which you will be able to quench all the fiery darts of the wicked one. And take the helmet of salvation, and the sword of the Spirit, which is the word of God; praying always with all prayer and supplication in the spirit, being watchful to this end with all perseverance and supplication for all the saints" (Ephesians 6:11-18).

Overcoming Temptation Through Faith

We all know that to go to war we need the armor that will protect us, as well as mental and physical preparation. That is why generals challenge their soldiers with strong words to confront the adversary with confidence and courage.

The Bible specifies the elements with which we must arm ourselves. They are:

1. The Helmet of Salvation

The helmet protects the head. It provides a covering for the Christian against every mental attack. The enemy is astute and knows very well that the mind is a vulnerable target. If he can capture our thoughts, it will be easy to conquer our will. He always tries to disguise his presence by making people think those thoughts come from themselves. If they accept this lie, the devil will get them outside of the will of God. Sometimes one feels so small and miserable, but that idea does not come from the Lord. It is that very same voice of the enemy that tries to make us feel bad, so bad that we feel incapable of accomplishing the work of God. Ask the Lord in prayer to be able to distinguish between the voice of God, the voice of the enemy, and your own voice. When there is fear, doubt and discouragement, we can conclude that it is the voice of the enemy speaking. Every thought of faith and joy can only come from God. Our mind must be controlled by God and the helmet of salvation is the guarantee that He is going to save us and protect us.

2. The Breastplate of Righteousness

The breastplate of righteousness is like a bullet-proof vest. Righteousness means to act correctly, that is, to behave according to the will of God. This way, the Lord himself takes up our protection in order to guard our feelings and emotions from traumatic experiences. Solomon the wise remarked: "Keep your heart with all diligence for out of it spring the issues of life" (Proverbs 4:23). Regrettably, many homes are completely unprotected because they have not realized that the man is the guardian and protector of the family. The adversary has managed to bind men with vices, inordinate passion, and evil desires, including greed. And as the Lord said, if the strong man is tied it would be very easy to plunder his family. The adversary's favorite target is the emotions, but, if we surrender them into the hands of God, there will be a great protection for the rest of the family.

We must understand that the adversary tries to hurt us through:

- Childhood trauma
- Family conflict/discord
- Emotional problems
- Unpleasant experiences with friends

The breastplate of righteousness signifies that God has forgiven and justified us, and that His grace surrounds us as a shield.

3. The Belt of Truth

The Word of God is His truth revealed to us bestowing salvation. We know that there is only one truth and everything outside of it is pure lies. As we understand that there is judgment for everyone who twists the truth, we cannot preach a lie as though it were God's absolute truth. The divine truth is revealed in the Word of God.

The Lord declared that Satan is the father of lies, and Paul said that we should put away lying and speak the truth with our neighbor.

If you were to place your words on a scale, what would you find? How many would be words of truth? How many would be contaminated with scheming or murmuring? A gossip is not only the one who speaks ill of his neighbor, but also the one who hears the rumor and indulges in it. Allowing a negative comment about someone is like opening our home to someone we have never seen before. He who often opens his door seeks ruin. Jesus said: "And you shall know the truth, and the truth shall make you free" (John 8:32). We will know the truth when the Word of God has taken root in our hearts and our lives revolve around it.

The Lord said through Moses: "And these words which I command you today shall be in your heart. You shall teach them diligently to your children, and shall talk to them when you sit in your house, when you walk by the way, when you lie down, and when you rise up. You shall bind them as a sign on your hand, and they shall be as frontlets between your eyes. You shall write them on the doorposts of your house and on your gates" (Deuteronomy 6:6-9).

When Joshua succeeded Moses in leadership, the Lord told him: "This Book of the Law shall not depart from your mouth, but you shall meditate in it day and night, that you may observe to do according to all that is written in it. For then you will make your way prosperous, and then you will have good success" (Joshua 1:8).

4. The Shield of Faith

The shield of faith protects us from all of the enemy's fiery darts.

"So then faith comes by hearing, and hearing by the word of God" (Romans 10:17).

God has given us the ability to believe in order to positively change our circumstances. To accomplish this, it is essential that we hear what God has to say about it, since everything we want to conquer must be backed up by the Word of God. The Word contains the seed of life, and when it falls into a heart that is healthy and full of faith, the seed sprouts and produces the fruit of the desired miracle. All the power of God is concentrated in His Word, and only our faith can activate it and put it into action. We must understand that our ears can hear many sounds, but our success in hearing the voice of God will depend on our attention to it. We must listen attentively to the voice of God so that He can accomplish His purpose through His powerful Word.

We must saturate our minds with the Word of God, which, through the years, has remained intact and retained its power. Just as powerful as the Word of God was in the time of the prophets, it is powerful in our days.

We must understand that the Word of God is not subject to time or space, because God is not subject to human laws. God established time for human beings.

His Word remains in the spiritual realm, and as always, that which is spiritual rules over that which is natural. Once it comes from the mouth of the Lord, His Word cannot return until it has fulfilled the purpose for which it was sent. That is, as long as there is one life willing to believe. This Word has to be present, fulfilling its mission in that life. Jesus already said: "Heaven and earth will pass away, but My words will by no means pass away" (Mark 13:31).

Faith in God becomes the most powerful protecting wall that you have ever had. It becomes a high place of refuge for your life. "Blessed is the man who listens to me, watching daily at my gates, waiting at the posts of my doors. For whoever finds me finds life, and obtains favor from the LORD, but he who sins against me wrongs his own soul; All those who hate me love death" (Proverbs 8:34-36).

We must understand that:
- Faith takes us beyond circumstances.
- Faith protects us from sudden and damaging attacks.
- Faith brings us closer to God.
- We obtain faith in the secret place of prayer.
- Faith takes us beyond our abilities.
- Faith causes us to dream and visualize.
- Faith and obedience to the Word of God protects us.

5. The Sword of the Spirit

The sword of the Spirit refers to the Word of God. It has come into our heart so that it can be confessed by our lips. Every word given by God is charged with power. The Greek word for "power" is "dynamis," from where we get the word "dynamite."

"The LORD thundered from heaven, and the Most High uttered His voice..." (Psalm 18:13). Just one word uttered under the anointing of the Holy Spirit activates the whole spiritual sphere in the heavenly places. God Himself will back His Word just as He did with the Lord Jesus.

With His word He cast out demons, calmed the winds, smoothed the waves, healed the sick, and raised the dead. God will do the same through the words that leave your mouth, because in His name, we will do greater things than Jesus.

The writer of Hebrews said: "For the word of God is living and powerful, and sharper that any two-edged sword, piercing even to the division of soul and spirit, and of joints and marrow, and is a discerner of the thoughts and intents of the heart" (Hebrews 4:12).

This is what happens when the Word of God is released through our lips. The Word is:

- *Living, hence it gives life*
Jesus said that the spirit gives life and the flesh profits nothing. The Word of God is spirit and life. The life of the Word of God is in the Spirit. If it did not have the backing of the Spirit of God, it would be devoid of power.

- *Powerful (Greek-"energes")*
This is: operational and dynamic. It is charged with divine energy and it fulfills the purpose for which God sent it. "So shall My word be that goes forth from My mouth; It shall not return to Me void, but it shall accomplish what I please, and it shall prosper in the thing for which I sent it" (Isaiah 55:11).

- *Sharper than a double-edged sword (Greek-"makhaira")*
It is like a surgeon's scalpel that is destined to heal. When the Word of God is released, it reaches the most intimate parts of the person, and like a sharp scalpel, it heals the

deepest wounds of the soul and the spirit. Double-edged (Greek-"distomos") literally means "having two mouths." This allows it to penetrate deeper–reaching joints and marrow–and it's able to discern the most secret thoughts and the intentions of the heart.

No word that proceeds out of the mouth of a servant of God is devoid of power. It must fulfill the purpose for which it was sent.

6. Feet Conditioned for the Gospel

The preaching of the gospel is one of the greatest blessings that God has bestowed upon us. Through it, we bring life and hope to people.

Be sure that the message that comes out of your lips goes out with the same anointing and strength as that of Jesus. I recommend you to:

- **Speak always of Jesus.** Your goal should be to bring all of those who hear you into a full relationship with Jesus Christ. When the Word of God is accepted into the heart, the Word of God becomes flesh in those lives, and becomes a part of the person receiving it.

- **Always motivate with your words.** One of the mistakes I made early in my ministry, was that in my zeal to get them to turn to God, I would speak to people in harsh words, as if scolding them. On several occasions I found myself in the middle of heated arguments and I never conceded to others. I wanted to win every argument, until I realized that it is better to lose an argument and win a soul than to win an argument and lose a soul.

- **Use a positive language.** Even though some use negative language to obtain something positive, I believe that it is always better to speak words that bring hope. My wife and I seize every opportunity we have with others, because we know that God has placed them in our path. We try, even if we only have a couple of minutes with them, to give an appropriate word to help in the decisions they need to make.

- **Let your words fill the void that people have in their emotions.** In general, people allow negative thoughts into their minds. These come in and take root in their emotions. A negative thought lurks behind inappropriate behavior. Many are battling guilt, fear, depression, loneliness, sadness, feelings of insecurity, etc. We must purpose in our hearts that each one of our words will be like a healing balm for the soul of those who listen to us, so that they may once again believe in themselves, in God and in others. This is why the author of Proverbs writes: "The lips of the righteous feed many..." (Proverbs 10:21).

- **Be resourceful in communicating effectively.** We are aware that as preachers we are in competition with television, but television does not have what we posses: the anointing of the

Holy Spirit of God. We must try to use good illustrations, parables, edifying testimonies, and whenever possible, the resources that technology offers.

Pray Without Ceasing

Paul asks that our prayer life be continual. The only thing that moves God's hand is the prayer made in supplication and faith for everything He places in our hearts. Maintaining a rich prayer life is allowing our soul to be continually filled with the presence of God. We know that the effectual, fervent prayer of a righteous man avails much. The Lord said: "Call to Me and I will answer you and show you great and mighty things, which you do not know" (Jeremiah 33:3).

Prayer implies entering into intimacy with God and drawing from His riches everything we need. Everything you need has already been created in the spiritual realm. Through intercession you enter into that spiritual realm and extract any blessing you need to obtain, and bring it into the natural realm where we live. Prayer has to be as persistent as that of Hannah who poured her heart out before the Lord, asking Him to grant her a child. Her prayer was like a walk down a long road, at the end of which, was the King of Glory. When she was in the temple praying, she was walking her last mile.

When she arose, it was because her request had definitively been placed in God's hands, and because of this, she was never sad again (see 1 Samuel 1:9-18).

What are the steps to follow in warfare?

1. Repentance for our sins, the sins of our family and the sins of the nation.
2. Perseverance.
3. Guidance from the Holy Spirit. You must read the Word before entering into warfare.
4. Pray with others who have the same purpose.
5. Winning the battle in our minds is the first step to overcome.

We must understand that God has given us valuable weapons for spiritual warfare, which we must use so we are not vulnerable to the enemy. The beginning of victory is to truly know who the enemy is, his purposes and strategies. This way we will know which weapons to use when he attacks.

"Lord, today I acknowledge that You alone are the One who guards and protects me. Help me to keep my eyes fixed on You because I do not want to ever fall or fail you. Give me the necessary faith to remain steadfast in You. Keep me from the plans the enemy has to seduce me with temptation, for I know he seeks to destroy me. Strengthen me in You. I put on the armor you have prepared for me, for I know that it will provide me with full victory in every aspect of my life. In the name of Jesus, Amen."

Chapter 9

HOW TO BE FREE FROM THE CURSE

"…Deliver us from evil…" (Matthew 6:13)

We are all victims of curse if we ignore what God has for us, but we receive His blessings when we listen to His voice and keep His Word by putting it into action.

One of the places where the believer has to battle is related to strongholds that have taken hold in their life because of past experiences.

Sometimes we are caught in the effects without evaluating the causes of the problems. Some couples wonder, "Why are things going wrong in our marriage? Why are we having so many struggles?" Others faced with their internal conflicts, keep asking, "Why am I so susceptible to temptation?" They do not know why they do the things they do not want to do, and allow influences by people who should not even be around them.

We must understand that a curse may be operating behind all of this. When Solomon said: "Like a flitting sparrow, like a flying swallow, so a curse without cause shall not alight" (Proverbs 26:2), he was referring to evil always having a source.

The first thing we must understand is that everything has an opposite. Just as good exists, evil exists. Just as God exists, there is also an evil and perverse being known as Satan. Just as God has an angelic hierarchy, made up of angels, archangels, seraphim and cherubim, the enemy has built his own government made up of principalities, powers, dark rulers of this world, and spiritual wickedness in the heavenlies. God wants to draw His children through love. The adversary attempts to control them through hate and violence. God gave us His Son Jesus Christ to give us salvation. The adversary comes to steal, kill and destroy. God yearns for all His children to know their rights and enjoy all their privileges. The adversary strives to make believers live in ignorance of all the blessings that God has prepared in advance for them.

Moving From Idolatry to Worshiping the True God

After the people of Israel left Egypt, God became their Shepherd. By the skillfulness of His hand, He led them through Moses. Shortly before the Israelites entered the Promised Land, Moses signaled that the elders must pronounce blessing from Mount Gerizim to cover all the people. In the same way, he arranged for six of them to go up Mount Ebal to pronounce a curse: "And the Levites will speak with a loud voice and say to all the men of Israel: Cursed is the one who makes a carved or molded image, an abomination to the LORD, the work of the hands of the craftsman, and sets it up in secret. And all the people shall answer and say, Amen" (Deuteronomy 27:14-15).

Adam had known a spiritual God, but because of his sin, his first reaction was to run from the presence of God. Then he tried by his own efforts, to find value within himself, and he made frontlets to cover his nudity. That was not enough, because these coverings covered his front, and not his back. It is that way with everything man does with the intention of competing with God. He can only see what is in front of his eyes, and he cannot go past that. The Lord had to intervene and make appropriate clothes from animal skin. God sacrificed innocent animals to give man clothing, and at the same time cover his shame.

What God did became a prototype of the redemption of man that would be accomplished centuries later when God would give His only Son as a sacrifice for the salvation of the human race. The Creator had to teach Adam the right way to relate to Him, which was through a substitutionary offering for his sins. God did not give Adam an image of a physical figure, because the God of heaven could not be compared to anything in this world. That is because all images belong to the world's system, but when man leaves his mortal body those images will not mean anything. The spiritual will absorb the earthly, and the eternal will rule over time and space.

When Solomon dedicated the temple, he prayed: "But will God indeed dwell on the earth? Behold heaven and the heaven of heavens cannot contain You. How much less this temple I have built?" (1 Kings 8:27).

King Solomon understood that God cannot be measured or limited in any way, and that no house, no matter how big, would be sufficient to give capacity to God. The Lord has always wanted for man to understand that idolatry, in whatever form, is a great offense to Him. God continually warns His people to avoid involving themselves in any kind of idolatry, because people lose their spiritual vision. "You shall not make for yourself a carved image; any likeness of anything that is in heaven above or that is in the earth; you shall not bow down to them or serve them. For I, the LORD your God, am a jealous God, visiting the iniquity of the fathers upon the children to the third and fourth generations of those who hate Me, but showing mercy to thousands, to those who love Me and keep My commandments" (Exodus 20:4-6). God's position against idolatry is so severe that in the second of the ten commandments of the Law He established for His people, He stipulated that the sin of idolatry would be punished even on the descendants of those who practice it for four generations. Idolatry is an abomination before God and those who practice it are His enemies; they are cursed and provoke His wrath. The apostle Paul counsels the believers of Corinth, saying: "Therefore, my beloved, flee from idolatry" (1 Corinthians 10:14).

This refers to images and physical representations that people revere or worship. It includes amulets, talismans, or whatever other objects might be acclaimed like a deity. God does not want us to make or represent His image in any form. We must understand that it is necessary for those who worship Him, to do it spirit and in truth. Idolatry is like spiritual adultery. Whoever worships God and also reveres another god is committing spiritual adultery. Commonly, the sin of idolatry is inherited from ancestors. We have had to renounce this sin because our parents were very idolatrous. Most of them were born into the Roman Catholic tradition, and we had to repent of everything they worshipped as God, but was not. We had to renounce many of the covenants that had been made and ask the Lord, in His mercy, to sanctify us and give us the opportunity to worship only Him in spirit and in truth. God gave us the privilege of being the first Christians in our family so that many of Claudia's relatives, and mine, might be set free from the curse of idolatry. First, we had to remove it from their hearts through faith, so that later they could leave it behind in a real way. We saw how they themselves took those images and destroyed them because they understood that they had put a veil on their eyes which prevented them from seeing the blessings of God in different areas of their lives.

When they destroyed their idols, the heavens opened and their hearts were ready to receive the gospel of life. The prophet Elisha understood that idolatry had contaminated the heavens of his nation and that it had caused the economy of the people to stagnate completely. Because of this sin, prosperity was completely absent from the nation. It was not until idolatry was broken that the heavens opened and people could shout: "The LORD, He is God, the LORD, He is God!" (1 Kings 18:39).

During the times of the apostles, the message Paul preached in the city of Ephesus, confronting idolatry, was very effective. The results were: "And many who had believed came confessing and telling their deeds. Also, many of those who had practiced magic brought their books together and burned them in the sight of all. And they counted up the value of them, and it totaled fifty thousand pieces of silver. So the word of the Lord grew mightily and prevailed" (Acts 19:18-20).

Breaking the Curse of Dishonor

"Cursed is the one who treats his father or his mother with contempt. And all the people shall say, Amen" (Deuteronomy 27:16).

"Behold, I will send you Elijah the prophet before the coming of the great and dreadful day of the LORD. And he will turn the hearts of the fathers to the children, and the children to their fathers, lest I come and strike the earth with a curse" (Malachi 4:5-6).

We are aware that the period we are living in is one where the family environment is in great crisis. However, God promised that something supernatural would happen in the end times through believers. I think that in the end times the Church will move to another dimension and be able to complete the Great Commission. God will give the persecuted believers the same anointing Elisha had: the anointing of reconciliation. When God gave us the Vision of the Government of Twelve, we began to feel that a hand of reconciliation fell over our ministry. People who attended the Encounters, left completely transformed. When we listened to the testimonies, each one expressed what God had done in their lives. We could see that the wounds the children had felt, mostly caused by their parents, were completely healed. One of them, crying, said, "Mom, I forgive you for abandoning me when I was a kid. Mom, you're not the bad woman I always thought you to be, even though I always thought the worst of you. Today, I know that you are a woman, human like all the rest of us. Whatever the motives you had for deciding to leave me, I don't judge you. I bless you and I forgive you. And if one day I meet you, I'll tell you that myself." Every curse that young person had put on her mother was canceled that day through the ministry of reconciliation.

Although the Bible says: "Cursed is he who dishonors his father or his mother…," we cannot ignore the fact that many children allow their hearts to be filled with hate and resentment towards their parents because of the unjust way they have been dealt with. Jesus understood this suffering because He Himself had to experience the rejection of the Heavenly Father.

On the other hand, there are also children who abuse the generosity of their parents, and who take a contemptuous attitude towards them. Solomon says: "Whoever curses his mother or father, his lamp will be put out in deep darkness" (Proverbs 20:20).

Never before in history, have human beings been as irreverent towards their parents as they are today. Children have practically risen up against their parents. In the time of Moses, when a son raised his voice at his father and used vulgarities with him, he was taken outside the camp and stoned. Today, children treat their parents like they were servants. Many of them have received big curses for the way they have treated their parents. Paul says: "Honor your father and mother, which is the first commandment with a promise; that it may be well with you and you may live long on the earth" (Ephesians 6:2-3).

Why is it that parents actions mark their children for life? We must understand that God made us in an integral way; the stability of our emotions is directly related to the affections of our parents. When parents fail in this area, they leave a huge void that only God's grace can fill. At one time, a friend shared with me what an encounter with his dad had been like. He had been abandoned when he was five. After forty-five years, he finally reached the dream of finding his father. He found out where he lived, and he arrived to surprise him. It was a meeting full of emotions, there were more tears and hugs than reproaches. After leaving the house my friend felt full. Finally, he was able to fill the emptiness that accompanied him for many years. What about those who never get to find their parents? Or those whose parents do not look after them? To them especially, God reveals Himself as the true Father. A while back a lady came to talk with my wife and I, and she opened her heart telling us how her father had wounded her deeply, and the things that had caused her pain in life. We ministered to her about the fatherly love of God, the glory of

God descended, and the whole place was full of His presence. She had a vision where she saw Jesus hanging on the Cross, and He showed her the wounds that were all suffered for her. She could not stop crying because she finally felt that her Father God was interested in her, and came down to heal each one of her wounds. She understood that the Lord is sufficient to fill our emotions.

Breaking the Curse of Oppression

"Cursed is the one who moves his neighbor's landmark. And all the people say, 'Amen!'" (Deuteronomy 27:17)

It is incredible that God has established that those who do not help those under their leadership develop to their full potential and grow in their capabilities, will fall under judgment and curse.

This group includes parents who limit their child's growth and who close the doors to the development of their lives. It also includes those whom God has placed in a privileged ministerial position, but do not allow their disciples to grow.

Perhaps you know believers who have so much fire inside of them, who speak so much of things from above that they give the impression of always being in the clouds, but there are also other believers, the ones whose minds are always focused on their problems and cannot find the time to solve them. This is where the leader has to demonstrate his ability; his goal must be to establish a healthy self-esteem in each one of his disciples. Whoever is haughty must be helped to come down a little, and whoever has a spirit of low self-esteem must be brought to a level where he can believe in himself, rising up in him the spirit of a conqueror. The Lord had to say to Peter: "What God has cleansed you must not call common" (Acts 10:15).

As far as Peter was concerned, the Gentiles did not have any hope of redemption since they were all contaminated by their pagan customs, but the Lord encourages the Apostle to see things differently. Thanks to Peter's obedience, the church among the Gentiles was born. I believe that one of the ways in which we can lift the curse from the people is through the work of cell groups. Many can easily come up with plenty of arguments against holding a cell group meeting because they think that Gentiles do not deserve it.

- Cornelius was a devout and God-fearing man, along with his household.
- He prepared the room to ensure the success of the meeting.
- His house became a door of blessing for the Church of Jesus Christ.
- Peter was an answer to Cornelius' prayers.
- Peter was able to envision the redemption of the Gentiles.
- Peter was obedient to the voice of God.
- Peter was sensitive to the message he had to deliver.
- His words were confirmed by the anointing of the Holy Spirit.

How to Be Free From the Curse

Breaking the Curse of Spiritual Blindness

"Cursed is the one who makes the blind to wander off the road" (Deuteronomy 27:18).

They are blind leaders of the blind. And if the blind leads the blind, both will fall into a ditch" (Matthew 15:14). Spiritual blindness is as exasperating as the lack of vision. I am convinced in my heart that God wants to use us believers, in these last days, as burning torches to carry the fire of God to the farthest corners of the world.

But in order to accomplish this, we must raise an army of brave men and women who are willing to pay the price so that the Kingdom of God might soon be established on this earth.

"I can see! I can see!" were the excited cries that came out of the mouth of this lady who attended a healing service led by one of my brothers in the city of Cúcuta, Colombia. Five years earlier, this woman had been hammering a nail onto a wall in her house; the nail broke loose and pierced one of her eyes. When they extracted the piece of metal, her intraocular fluid came out. Her eye became a whitish color, and she lost her vision. During the time of ministration, her faith increased and she felt a strong heat in her eye. What a pleasant surprise it was as she covered the good eye to confirm that the other had been healed! The Lord performed a complete miracle returning not only her vision, but the beauty of her original eye.

When they asked the blind man whom Jesus healed, "What did he do?" He said, "The only thing I know is that I was blind and now I see" (John 9:25).

God wants to provide us with sight, not only in the natural, but in the spiritual realm as well. He who does not have his spiritual eyes open is blind, and "the people perish without a vision." Where there is no vision, the people lack restraint.

Jesus formed an army of brave men who were capable of wielding spiritual weapons. He began by raising twelve men who burned with the fire of the Holy Spirit; twelve men of prayer saturated with the presence of Jesus; twelve men who saw the glory of God through Jesus Christ. We are privileged to participate in the same blessing by becoming a part of that same army of spiritual warriors that will take the nations for God.

Years ago, as I was praying for a strategy that would help take the cellular Vision to the entire church, the Lord Himself asked me: "How many people did Jesus Christ train?" In my mind, I surveyed the different phases of Jesus' life and I found that although He preached to the crowds that followed Him, He had concentrated all His efforts on just twelve men. Jesus provided them with skills; He trained to carry on the work of the ministry. God persisted: "If you follow My Son's example and train twelve, then those twelve train twelve, and those twelve train twelve more, and so on, the growth will be unprecedented." With that revelation, I understood that God was placing the vision of government in my hands. "For the earth shall be filled with the knowledge of the glory of the LORD, as the waters cover the sea" (Habakkuk 2:14).

The Lord tells the prophet that a vision of government is coming for the end times and that it will be bestowed upon those of humble hearts. Then it adds, that when the vision finds a home in the heart of the believers, it will flood the earth as the waters cover the sea.

To establish the G12 Vision, it is important to:

a. **Accept the Vision by faith.** In faith, it is not man's logic that prevails, but rather divine logic. In the same manner Mary conceived Jesus in her womb. She did it because she believed the angel's words. Because of her faith, she was able to see the miracle before it took place and she was able to say: "Let it be to me according to your word" (Luke 1:28-35).

b. **Understand that the leader is the key.** The Vision must enter into each one of our hearts so that we can be saturated in it. It must be made known because everyone will do that which the leader does. The leader must be sensitive to the voice of the God; he must learn to hear His voice. This requires a greater commitment in prayer, and a higher degree of holiness. The leader must allow the Holy Spirit to take complete control of his or her life.

c. **Obedience must be complete and not partial.** "Leave your tradition…" (Genesis 12:1). When God spoke these words, He was not telling Abram to leave only ninety-nine percent of his tradition and to keep some. God's intention was for Abram to leave everything behind. However, the patriarch obeyed only in part. He left his family, but took Lot along with him. While they remained together, Abram was not able to see the vision; he had a veil covering his eyes. If you obey only in part, that disobedience will become a veil over your life and ministry.

d. **The leader must have a healed heart.** By the power of the Holy Spirit, God heals the deep wounds in the heart of man. That is how Abraham came to know the Lord as El-Shaddai (see Genesis 17:1). "El" means "almighty," and "Shad" means "breast," referring to a mother's breast; to the cradling in the mother's bosom. With this revelation, God was healing the patriarch's heart as though telling him: "Abraham, your father failed you, but I am the One who does not fail, because there is nothing impossible for Me. If your mother did not nurture you with the right teachings, I am giving you from My breast all you need."

Restoring the Blessing of Sexuality

We know that sexuality was created by God, and it is blessed within divine parameters. God Himself gave man sexual enjoyment, but when man moves away from God, his sexual life becomes completely distorted. We must understand that we live in difficult days. Man is Satan's target and he is using every means to pervert the mind. Every film, every magazine, every song, every image transmitted over the Internet contains a message of mental slavery. Seeking to make man think that sexual impurity is a normal part of life, and that it is impossible to live in righteousness and integrity. Satan wears down the mind of man with this continuous bombardment. It is a psychological attack meant to weaken man, to tire him, and to make him think that he cannot fight against temptation. It is meant to convince him that temptation is stronger than he is, making him surrender to his desires. The Scripture says: "No temptation has overtaken you except such as is common to man; but God is faithful, who will not allow you to be tempted beyond what you are able, but with the temptation will also make the way of escape, that you may be able to bear it" (1 Corinthians 10:13). There is always "a way of escape" for man to be free of sexual oppression.

Breaking the Curse of Injustice

"Cursed is the one who perverts the justice due the stranger, the fatherless and the widow. And all the people shall say, Amen!" (Deuteronomy 27:19)

The weak are those who cannot defend themselves or who are in a position of disadvantage.

In that group, we can include: foreigners, orphans and widows. There is one more group we need to consider: unborn babies in their mothers' wombs who desire to be given the chance to be born. No one is as defenseless as a developing baby. How many couples agree to go through abortions? This is an injustice toward the weak.

Years ago, a couple came to me for a blessing, because they had decided to get an abortion. When I questioned their decision, they said that they had too many children and they could not financially support another one. I then explained about the sin of abortion. This couple accepted the counsel, received the light of the Word of God, and on that day repented and renounced to every thought of abortion. A few months later, a baby girl was born who brought much joy into their home. Presently, that young lady is a youth leader in her church. There are parents who kill the hope of their descendants. The Psalmist said: "Lord, keep me from bloodshed." It doesn't matter if you went to bed with a young lady and want to cover your sin. If you consented to an abortion, there is a curse on your life, and the blood of that child cries out for vengeance. Only the blood of Christ can break that curse.

Breaking the Curse of Inappropriate Sexuality

Adam and Eve are standing before the tree of the knowledge of good and evil. A few moments prior, God had placed them there, pure and innocent and covered by a robe of holiness. In the next scene, the Lord is looking for them in the garden and cannot find them. His voice shakes the whole universe. It carries as much authority as when Christ told Lazarus who was already dead for four days, to come out of the grave. God's voice pierces the heavens, reaches the dwelling of the first couple, and asks three questions. He asks these same questions of us today.

1. *Where is your sexuality?*

"Where are you?" (Genesis 3:9). When he received instructions from God, Adam never suspected that he would have to confront a spiritual force that would try to seduce him into disobeying the divine command. It is important to understand that at that moment Adam was predominantly a spiritual being who, with his word of authority, could destroy any of the adversary's schemes. The enemy, however, was very cunning and foresaw all of this. He did not approach man in an aggressive or challenging way. Rather, he astutely chose the most charming and cunning creature in the garden. Through Eve, he managed to establish a dialogue, and softly carried them to the trap he had set for them. That was one of the saddest days for God. The man He had created to be like His own son, the one created in His image and likeness, had sinned.

That day, the heavens shook, the angels cried, and God was saddened because the spirit of His son had died as a result of sin. Satan had managed to turn the first couple's gaze toward the tree of which God had prohibited. He caused them to envision it differently until he encouraged them to rebel against God. They were willing to eat of the forbidden fruit with no regard for consequences. As a result, they now found themselves outside the divine garden in enemy territory, aware of their shame and completely vulnerable. This is like an analogy of the parable of the lost son, who flees his own home thinking that a better life waited him. They received the thoughts the enemy threw at them; the false notions that in order to enjoy the world they had to rebel against every kind of law. And in doing so, they would find greater pleasure.

The results were completely unexpected. It was as though they had fallen into a bottomless pit; their situation grew worse. Until a merciful light illuminated their understanding and they were able to reconsider their situation.

They heard the voice of the Father calling, "Where are you?" This caused them to seek a second chance, and the Father granted it. Presently, the Heavenly Father calls you and says, "Son, where is your sexuality?" It does not matter how far you have gone, what mistakes you have made, or if you have mishandled your sexuality. God wants to give you a second chance.

God had to prompt David through the prophet Nathan to turn back to Him. David came to be known as the sweet cantor of Israel. He had a pure and innocent heart, but everything in him changed overnight. He began to commit the most heinous sins, all because of incorrect visualizations. From his royal palace, and while resting on his balcony, he saw a very beautiful woman undressing to bathe in the river. A powerful desire to be with her was awakened in him. Without regard for anything else, he took her, satisfied his own desire, and then sent her away. When he found out she was pregnant, and to cover his own sin, he had her husband killed and then married her. But the voice of the Lord came to David saying: "Why have you despised the commandment of the LORD, to do evil in His sight? You have killed Uriah the Hittite with the sword; you have taken his wife to be your wife, and have killed him with the sword of the people of Ammon. Now therefore, the sword shall never depart from your house, because you have despised Me, and have taken the wife of Uriah the Hittite to be your wife" (2 Samuel 12:9-10). David's sexuality was in the wrong place with his neighbor's wife. This resulted in serious consequences which affected his descendants.

When he put his own desires over the Word of God, he opened the door to a curse, allowing the adversary to raise up strong arguments against the royal family. David had to confront his sin when he saw death wrench his new born son. He could not do any thing to stop it. He had to confess before Nathan the prophet: "I have sinned." Even though David's transgression was grave, God extended His mercy and decided to forgive and restore him.

Something similar happens today. The enemy places in man an incontrollable desire for that which is forbidden. He makes him believe that sin is not that bad, and little by little takes him to an inappropriate visualization. Then he seizes an opportune moment to pull him away from the perfect place, the will of God. Man finds himself in the middle of rejection, shame, and the humiliation of having placed his sight on that which did not belong to him.

2. Who has been your teacher?

God wanted to hear from Adam's mouth where he had received the information concerning his sexuality. Hence the question: "Who told you that you were naked?" (Genesis 3:11). The apostle James said: "Do not be deceive, my beloved brethren. Every good gift and every perfect gift is from above, and comes down from the Father of lights, with whom there is no variation or shadow of turning" (James 1:16-17). There are only two sources from which we can receive information about sexuality: one comes from the Father of lights who does not waver in His opinions or changes His mind, and the other comes from error accompanied by seduction and deceit.

A while ago, a woman asked me to speak with her husband, because she had discovered that when alone, he was being seduced by pornography. Even though initially he tried to cover his wrongdoing, the evidence was so conclusive that he had to confess. When I asked him about the origins of this bad habit, he answered: "It was because of my parents' abandonment. I came to hate my mother so intensely that I started to watch how low a woman could get to justify in my mind that my mother was a bad woman. Hatred for my mother pushed me to take pornography as my teacher." That day, this man was able to forgive his mother and was able to uproot the hatred from his heart. God gave him great freedom in his spiritual life. He restored him, his home and his sexual life. That day a curse was broken that had been with him since childhood. Today this man uses his personal experience to help in the restoration of other homes, and to minister freedom to men who are going through the same situation.

King Solomon said: "For the commandment is a lamp, and the law a light; reproofs of instruction are the way of life, to keep you from the evil woman, from the flattering tongue of a seductress. Do not lust after her beauty in your heart, nor let her allure you with her eyelids. For by means of a harlot a man is reduced to a crust of bread; and an adulteress will prey upon his precious life" (Proverbs 6:23-26). We must understand that the teaching we receive from God is the right source; the one that will provide us with light. Each one of the parameters established by Him has the purpose of teaching us and protecting us from error. The enemy is ready to ensnare using evil women, the seduction of another woman, and the beauty of the harlot. The adversary's only goal is to trap a man's soul. If he succeeds, he will take away his strength to conquer. Then, that man will leave his home completely unprotected so the enemy can have his way with his wife, his children, and even his own life.

On the other hand, the writer of Proverbs tells us: "Let your fountain be blessed, and rejoice with the wife of your youth, as a loving deer and a graceful doe, let her breasts satisfy

you at all times; and always be enraptured with her love"
(Proverbs 5:18-19). Sexuality, within the parameters
established by God, produces great satisfaction. Only those
who heed the divine laws will come to know it. Everyone
who makes the Holy Spirit His teacher will never have guilt,
remorse, frustration or bitterness, because God will bless every
area of his life.

History tells us of times when mankind lost its bearings
and restraint giving in to impure desires. For that reason,
God decided to eliminate them, but there was a man named
Noah who found grace in the eyes of the Lord. Because of
this man and his testimony, God decided to extend His mercy
to mankind. He only needs one man who will swim against
the current of this world; someone who will make a faithful
covenant with Him. Through this man, God will judge
the city, the nation and the world. Many will remark, "It's
impossible to live a life of holiness." But God, through us, has
a message for each of them: "You are wrong. Here's my child
who has been able to live a holy life, in righteousness and who
has believed My Word. I will judge the world through them.
In the same manner that Noah judged the world through a life
of holiness, God will do the same through each one of us.

Before the people of Israel went to possess the Promised
Land, God gave them the following warning: "When you come
into the land which the LORD your God is giving you, you
shall not learn to follow the abominations of those nations"

(Deuteronomy 18:9). For the people who lived in Canaan, no moral values existed. They had all given in to lasciviousness, and were carried away into the most abominable practices. That was one of the main reasons God decided to evict those nations from before the people of Israel. The Lord asked the people of Israel to remain holy because a holy God could only relate with those who lived in the same level of holiness.

3. What have you done?

One day, each person will be confronted by God to give an account of their deeds. The first couple had to present themselves before God to explain their disobedience.

In the days of the prophet Daniel, King Belshazzar was confronted by the Lord in the middle of one of his banquet celebrations because he had used the sacred vessels brought from the temple of God in Jerusalem for his pagan party. He had a vision of a hand that wrote on the wall. Daniel was the only one able to interpret the writing on the wall. He told the king that the hand responsible for the writing had been sent from the presence of God. "Mene, Mene, Tekel Upharsin."

The interpretation is as follows:
- MENE: God has numbered your kingdom, and ended it;
- TEKEL: You have been weighed in the balances, and found wanting;
- PERES: Your kingdom has been divided, and given to the Mcdcs and Persians" (Daniel 5:24-28).

When God demanded an account from this king, He found nothing to justify his staying any longer on this earth so He put an end to his days. King Belshazzar never imagined that that very night God would call his deeds into account.

Unfortunately, there are many living in this world as though they will never have to give an account to God. Nevertheless, there are two appointments no one will be able to miss. The first one is with death, and the second is with the divine court. Our eternal destiny will depend on that last appointment.

Paul said: "This I say, therefore, and testify in the Lord, that you should no longer walk as the rest of the Gentiles walk, in the futility of their mind, having their understanding darkened, being alienated from the life of God, because of the ignorance that is in them, because of the blindness of their heart" (Ephesians 4:17-18).

"And you He made alive, who were dead in trespasses and sins, in which you once walked according to the course of this world, according to the prince of the power of the air, the spirit who now works in the sons of disobedience, among whom also we all once conducted ourselves in the lusts of our flesh, fulfilling the desires of the flesh and of the mind, and were by nature children of wrath, just as the others" (Ephesians 2:1-3).

If God were to ask you: "What have you done with your sexual life?" How would you answer Him? At the conclusion of a marriage conference, a couple came over to talk to me. The man told me: "Pastor, I have a problem that I haven't been able to share with anyone, and it has to do with my sexual life." After listening to his confession, we got to the root of the matter and discovered that it all had originated from his childhood. When this man was able to bring an account of his deeds to God, the curse that had tormented him was removed from his life and he experienced a great deliverance. Many people are fighting the biggest battles of their lives in this area, not understanding that they need help and that the best help can only come from God. We must understand that those who give their lives over to sexual promiscuity generally end up alone and full of affliction.

Solomon said: "Remove your way far from her, and do not go near the door or her house, lest you give your honor to others, and your years to the cruel one; lest aliens be filled with your wealth, and your labors go to the house of a foreigner; and you mourn at last, when your flesh and your body are consumed, and say, 'How I have hated instruction, and my heart despised correction! I have not obeyed the voice of my teachers, nor inclined my ear to those who instructed me! I was on the verge of total ruin, in the midst of the assembly and congregation'" (Proverbs 5:8-14).

The writer's warning is: "Distance your way from her." This implies having self-discipline and a decision to end every inappropriate relationship; to cut away from the past never to return, not even in your mind, because continuing in an inappropriate relationship will bring disastrous consequences to your life and your family. Generally the ones who stay trapped are the ones who close their ears to counsel and prefer to leave the church which was their only source of protection.

THE CROSS SETS US FREE FROM THE CURSE.

What is the meaning of the Cross? If we were to ask a Jew about his concept of the Cross, he would probably say it was a cursed place where the most abominable criminals of the nation died.

If the Cross is a symbol of a curse, how is it also the most important symbol of blessing. When the first couple sinned in the Garden of Eden, there were several trees, but there were two that stood out: the tree of life and the tree of the knowledge of good and evil. If man ate of the tree of life, he would live forever; he would be like the angels that never die. And if the man took of the fruit of the knowledge of good and evil, both physical and spiritual death would come. Man chose the tree of the knowledge of good and evil and ate its fruit, and for that reason, God put him out of paradise. He found himself in the desert with affliction, infirmity, pain, poverty, ruin and loneliness. Man began to live out the effects of his own sin, and this is where the doors were opened to all the evil that affects your life.

God had to establish another tree, a different tree, a tree with two beams; one vertical that looked toward God, and one horizontal that looked toward the needs of man. This tree is the Cross. What does the Cross signify?

The apostle Paul said he had been crucified to the world and the world to him (see Galatians 6:14). Jesus never knew sin, but on the Cross He absorbed all curse for us. He became a magnet that attracted our curses. Generational curses began to be attracted to Him on the Cross. Jesus went to the Cross, not for any sin He had committed, nor for any sinful practices of His own. No! Jesus went to the Cross to take your place and mine.

Everyone without exception has taken the way of the world; the way of sin. But God took our sin and placed it on the life of Jesus, and allowed Him to go to the Cross as a curse to take the place of a fallen, perverse, and utterly sinful race. Jesus took our place. It was a cross because the Cross symbolizes the curse.

There Jesus went and He was not dying as the blessed one of God, but as a nation, a people, a cursed and perverse generation, separated from God. Jesus was receiving the punishment for all of mankind, and with love saying: "You're not going to die. I'm taking your place. I accept your curse. I submit to the Cross. I die crucified.

Paul wrote to the Galatians: "Christ has redeemed us from the curse of the law, having become a curse for us, for it is written: 'Cursed is everyone who hangs on a tree'" (Galatians 3:13). Earlier he confessed: "I have been crucified with Christ; it is no longer I, who live, but Christ who lives in me and the life I now live in the flesh, I live by faith in the Son of God who loved me and gave himself for me" (Galatians 2:20).

We must understand that we all like sheep have gone astray, and each one chose his own way. So God, to redeem us, had to put the weight of our sins on the shoulders of His Son, Jesus Christ.

When Jesus went to the Cross of Calvary, He was carrying the entire consequence of the curse. Isaiah said: "From the sole of the foot even to the head, there is no soundness in it, but wounds and bruises and putrefying sores; they have not been closed or bound up, or soothed with ointment" (Isaiah 1:6). There can be no greater display of love than what God gave to us through the sacrifice of His only Son. To anyone who understands this teaching and returns to Jesus with their whole heart, God will grant a miracle in their life. He will take all the curses of that person and put them onto the body of His Son, Jesus Christ.

Jesus Took Your Emotional Crisis

When God created us, He made us with emotions and feelings, but we know that because of sin, the adversary has astutely come to wound people in the depths of their hearts. We know that, in general, he uses those people nearest to us, so the wound would be deeper. In chapter twenty-eight of Deuteronomy, the Lord emphasizes the consequences that come from disobedience to the Word.

It is important that you understand that in spite of the fact a curse has been put in place because of the sin of man, through the revelation of the Cross, the curse can be removed; not only from your life, but from the lives of those dearest to you.

In the following verses of Deuteronomy chapter eighteen, you will find fourteen areas where the curse comes to attack our emotions, intellect, and actions. You will also be able to see that all of this was removed by God through the sacrifice of His Son, Jesus Christ.

Deuteronomy 28:20

- **Jehovah will send a curse against you.** "Christ redeemed us from the curse of the law when he died crucified" (Galatians 3:13).
- **Breakdown.** "The LORD is near to those who have a broken heart, and saves such as have a contrite spirit" (Psalm 34:18).
- **Failure in all that you set your hand to do.** "Just as many were astonished at you, so His visage was marred more than any man and His form more than the sons of men; so shall He sprinkle many nations. Kings shall shut their

mouths at Him; for what had not been told them they shall see, and what they had not heard they shall consider" (Isaiah 52:14-15).

- **Until you are destroyed and you perish quickly.** "With long life I will satisfy him and show him my salvation" (Psalm 91:16).

Deuteronomy 28:28

- **Madness.** Jesus said: "Come to Me, all you who labor and are heavy laden, and I will give you rest. Take my yoke upon you and learn from Me, for I am gentle and lowly in heart, and you will find rest for your souls. For My yoke is easy and my burden is light" (Matthew 11:28-30).
- **Blindness.** Jesus took our blindness: "My face is flushed from weeping, and on my eyelids is the shadow of death" (Job 16:16).
- **Panic stricken.** "Thus says the LORD and your God, who pleads the cause of his people: 'See, I have taken out of your hand the cup of trembling, the dregs of the cup of My fury; You shall no longer drink it'" (Isaiah 51:22).

Deuteronomy 28:34

- **So you shall be driven mad because of the sight which your eyes see.** "And the peace of God, which surpasses all understanding, will guard your hearts and minds through Christ Jesus" (Philippians 4:7).

Deuteronomy 28:65

- **And among those nations you shall find no rest.** "All we like sheep have gone astray; we have turned, every one, to his own way; And the LORD has laid on Him the iniquity of us all" (Isaiah 53:6).
- **Nor shall the sole of your foot have a resting place.** "He was oppressed and He was afflicted, yet he opened not His mouth; He was led as a lamb to the slaughter, And as a sheep before its shearers is silent, So he opened not His mouth" (Isaiah 53:7).
- **But there the LORD will give you a trembling heart.** "I sought the LORD, and He heard me, and delivered me from all my fears" (Psalm 34:4).
- **Failing eyes.** "I would have lost heart, unless I had believed that I would see the goodness of the LORD in the land of the living. Wait on the LORD; be of good courage, and He shall strengthen your heart; Wait, I say, on the LORD" (Psalm 27:13-14).
- **Anguish of the soul.** "Have mercy on me, Oh LORD, for I am in distress; my eye wastes away with grief, yes my soul and my body! For my life is spent with grief, and the years with sighing; my strength fails because of my iniquity, and my bones waste away. I am a reproach among all my enemies, but especially among my neighbors, and am repulsive to my acquaintances; those who see me outside flee from me" (Psalm 31:9-11).

Deuteronomy 28:66
- **Your life shall hang in doubt before you.** "I will be glad and rejoice in Your mercy, for You have considered my trouble; you have known my soul in adversities, and have not shut me up into the hand of the enemy; you have set my feet in a wide place" (Psalm 31:7-8).

Jesus Took Our Infirmities

All the curse of sickness fell upon the body of the Lord Jesus. He was made a curse for us so we could be healed of every infirmity and ailment. "Surely He has borne our grief and carried our sorrows; yet we esteemed Him stricken, smitten by God and afflicted. But He was wounded for our transgressions, He was bruised for our iniquities; the chastisement for our peace was upon Him, and by His stripes we are healed" (Isaiah 53:4-5).

Deuteronomy 28:21, 22, 27, 35 and 59, speak to us about 15 areas of health that are affected.

1. Mortality
2. Consumption
3. Fever
4. Inflammation
5. Severe Burning Fever
6. Scorching
7. Sudden Calamity
8. Mildew

9. Boils of Egypt
10. Tumors
11. Scabs
12. Rashes, from which you cannot be healed
13. Severe boils on your knees and legs, from the soles of your feet to the top of your head
14. Great plagues on you and your descendants
15. Serious and prolonged illness

During His ministry, the Lord Jesus healed all the sick. "But when Jesus knew it He withdrew from there. And great multitudes followed Him, and He healed them all" (Matthew 12:15). His healing power was such, that people just wanted to touch Him. "...and begged that they might only touch the hem of His garment. And as many as touched it were made perfectly well" (Matthew 14:36). "When evening had come, they brought to Him many who were demon-possessed. And He cast out the spirits with a word and healed all who were sick, that it might be fulfilled which was spoken by Isaiah the prophet, saying: 'He Himself took our infirmities and bore our sickness'" (Matthew 8:16-17).

I have the absolute certainty that anyone who seeks a miracle through the revelation of the Cross will get it.

I have seen more people healed and set free from understanding the revelation of the Cross, more than any other message. The interesting thing about the revelation of the Cross, is that even though it is a historic fact that happened two thousand years ago, its effectiveness is permanent and it is as if it happened today. Remember that in the spiritual realm, time and space do not exist. Everything is in an eternal state. For that reason, God took the spirits of the prophets of old and transferred them to the spiritual realm, where they were able to unite their spirits with the Spirit of Christ and prophesy the prayers made by Jesus while He was on the tree. In the same way, if we are able to enter into the spiritual realm, God would take our spirit and unite it with the Spirit of Christ and would show us conquering victories through His redemption. If in an act of faith, you could go to the Cross of Jesus Christ and leave all your burdens there, you could begin a new day, full of peace and blessing.

When someone is far from God, the enemy attacks him physically. Do not accept sickness in your body, nor in the body of your relatives. My mother is 83 years old and enjoys very good health, but each time she came back from a doctor visit, was depressed and sad. One day I asked her: "Are you sure you went to the doctor today?" And she answered, saying: "Yes, and he found me to be doing so poorly." I told her, "Mom, the divine doctor says you are not sick that all sickness and infirmity He took on Himself on the Cross of Calvary and you are healed by it." Later, I prayed for her and the bad feelings disappeared from her body immediately.

Jesus is the Solution for Family Crisis

We know that family crisis has increased in many homes, and that the majority of parents do not know how to handle the situation, but the answers are certainly found in the Word of God.

"Cursed shall be the fruit of your body and the produce of your land, the increase of your cattle and the offspring of your flocks. Cursed shall you be when you come in and cursed shall you be when you go out" (Deuteronomy 28:18-19).

"You shall beget sons and daughters, but they shall not be yours; for they shall go into captivity" (Deuteronomy 28:41).

This is the prevalent situation in many homes, where parents have trouble relating to their children. Many parents feel as though their children are strangers, or children feel resentment against their parents. Malachi the prophet said that in the end times, God would restore the anointing of Elijah, which is the anointing of family restoration. On this basis, God would make the heart of the parents turn to the children and the heart of the children turn to the parents (see Malachi 4:6). It is a genuine conversion of one toward the other.

When Deuteronomy says: "You shall beget sons and daughters, but they shall not be yours; for they shall go into captivity." What is it referring to? How many fathers hurt today when they see their children enslaved to drugs, alcohol, pornography, sexual impurity, drug trafficking and illicit businesses? This is slavery, and a life in captivity. God says that the anointing He brings breaks those chains and bonds, bringing freedom to the whole family.

Jesus Gives Us Victory in Our Finances

The desire of God's heart is that His children not experience financial difficulties. These come however, for different reasons, especially by ignoring the Word of God. Deuteronomy speaks to the issue in chapter 28:17, 29, 47, and 48. We can identify seven areas where evil attacks finances:

1. "Cursed shall be your basket and your kneading bowl." There is a curse over your family basket.
2. "You shall not prosper in your ways."
3. "You shall be oppressed." Much of that oppression will come from debts.
4. "You shall be plundered continually." Without your notice, a spirit of ruin will continually plunder your finances.
5. "No one shall save you."
6. "Because you did not serve the LORD your God with joy and gladness of heart for the abundance of everything." There will be a curse on your life because you do not serve Him with joy, and do not love His work.
7. "You shall serve your enemies." How? Through hunger, thirst, nakedness and lack.

It took the Lord five days of creation to prepare, down to the last detail, everything man would need so that he would lack nothing. God was so generous with man, that in creation itself, He provided for coming generations. So much that, on planet earth, there are enough natural resources for everyone to live like a king.

All these riches were affected by sin, but on the Cross of Calvary, Christ carried on His brow all the misery and ruin that had plagued mankind for centuries.

All of God's blessings were reserved for the seed of Abraham. Jesus purchased those legal rights and became the Owner of that inheritance. He shares it with those who have decided to fully surrender their lives to Him. Through faith in Jesus, we too can receive the legal rights to participate in that inheritance. "Ah, the smell of my son is like the smell of a field that the LORD has blessed. May God give you of heaven's dew and of earth's richness—and abundance of grain and new wine. May nations serve you and peoples bow down to you. Be lord over your brothers, and may the sons of your mother bow down to you. May those who curse you be cursed and those who bless you be blessed" (Genesis 27:27-29, NIV).

We can see that this really is a complete blessing where all aspects including physical, financial, business, family, emotional and spiritual are supplied.

"Heavenly Father, I thank you for Jesus; for on the Cross of Calvary my curse was completely cancelled. Today, I confess that by Jesus' stripes my whole body is healed. I believe that in the crown of thorns You bore my ruin and my poverty. Each one of Your nails delivered me from the guilt, oppression and shame that my sins produced. Beloved Father, I know that as I obey Your voice daily, I will be blessed in every area of my life and I will be able to enjoy the riches of the earth. I believe that Your all-encompassing blessing reaches me. In Jesus' name, Amen."

Chapter 10

GOD HAS DOMINION OVER ALL THINGS

"...for Yours is the kingdom, and the power, and the glory, forever and ever. Amen." (Matthew 6:13)

G od is the highest authority in the entire universe. Nothing exists that is above His authority.

The hearts of all the kings of the earth are in His hand and they are inclined towards what He wills. God has the power to crown kings and dethrone them. The Lord Jesus told Pilate that he would not have any power over Him if it had not been given from above by God. Those who govern the nations are only a reflection of the spiritual condition of their inhabitants.

God wants to raise up people who fear Him, and who understand His divine will and His plan to govern human beings. But once this is known, it must be accepted and expanded.

Even though Jesus died in weakness, He rose again in power, and all tribes, tongues, and nations were turned over to Him. He obtained dominion in the heavenly places and on the earth. Principalities and authorities are under His feet. He reigns over all, and His reign will never end.

Moses prayed: "Lord, You have been our refuge from generation to generation. Before the mountains were brought forth, You had formed the earth and the world, even from everlasting to everlasting, You are God" (Psalm 90:1-2).

And in one of the best known psalms among Christians, he says: "He who dwells in the secret place of the Most High, shall abide under the shadow of the Almighty. I will say of the LORD, 'He is my refuge and my fortress; My God, in Him I will trust.' Surely He shall deliver you from the snare of the fowler and from the perilous pestilence. He shall cover you with His feathers, and under His wings you shall take refuge; His truth shall be your shield and buckler. You shall not be afraid of the terror by night, nor of the arrow that flies by day, nor of the pestilence that walks in darkness nor of the destruction that lays waste at noonday" (Psalm 91:1-6). This entire psalm speaks of the protection that God gives to those who have made Him their refuge.

The desire of God's heart has been that man would raise up a generation for Him. He begins with the married couple, and later includes the entire family. That family joins other families, extending itself through social levels. From them must come people suitable to represent them in different levels of society.

But has man been able to govern this world? Could he survive without the help of God? Jesus Christ said: "...for without Me you can do nothing" (John 15:5).

From the beginning, God established His government in all creation: "In the beginning God created the heavens and the earth. The earth was without form and void and darkness was upon the face of the deep. And the Spirit of God was hovering over the face of the waters. Then God said, 'Let there be light,' and there was light " (Genesis 1:1-3). If God could transform chaos into something productive, He can make whatever changes He wants in our nations. He created this vast universe with the same perfection and symmetry as an expert watchmaker. For many years, it has been taught from pulpits that politics and Christianity are incompatible. By this means, men who have no fear of God become those who govern and establish laws according to their own thinking.

King Solomon said: "When the righteous are in authority, the people rejoice; but when a wicked man rules, the people groan" (Proverbs 29:2). It is hard to look at the world and find a nation that has not been contaminated at some point by the evil of the age: Corruption.

The last word of instruction from the Lord to His disciples was: "Go therefore and make disciples of all the nations, baptizing them in the name of the Father and of the Son, and of the Holy Spirit, teaching them to observe all things that I have commanded you; and lo, I am with you always, even to the end of the age" (Matthew 28:19-20).

We Can Be an Influence for Change

The government of Christ was first established in individuals, the apostles, who in less than a century, had transformed the world with the gospel.

The Thessalonians said of them: "These who have turned the world upside down have come here too" (Acts 17:6).

The Jews who accused Paul before Felix said of him: "For we have found this man a plague, a creator of dissension among all the Jews throughout the world, and a ringleader of the sect of the Nazarenes" (Acts 24:5).

Those apostles were ready to give up everything, even their own lives, to establish the Kingdom of God on earth. They gained strength by breaking the molds of paganism that had been established in different nations. The work the apostles had started was continued by the disciples they established in different nations. These, like those before them, were set on establishing the Kingdom of God on earth. Some sealed their testimony of faith in the flames fire, others were torn into pieces by the lions in the Roman Coliseum, others were imprisoned and lost their lands or died by the sword. All those first century believers had only one purpose in their hearts: to establish the Kingdom of God on the earth. This is the reason why in just three centuries, the most violent empire of the ages, the Roman Empire, was converted to Christianity in its totality.

One of the fundamental goals of those believers was to take the gospel to political leaders. With this motive Paul appealed to Cesar, who was the highest political authority of the time. Today we must strengthen ourselves by walking in the footsteps of the apostles, and without fear, try to conquer the political leadership of every nation for the glory of Jesus Christ.

We Must Decide Who Will Govern Us

The Lord said: "You are the salt of the earth; but if the salt loses its flavor, how shall it be seasoned? It is then good for nothing but to be thrown out and trampled underfoot by men" (Matthew 5:13). Salt is useful for preventing decay. Believers in important positions, whether political or in private industry, have to be that salt and not allow themselves to be seduced by power, fame or riches, and they must never lose sight of their purpose: to establish the Kingdom of God on the earth. When Paul wrote to Timothy, he said: "Therefore I exhort first of all that supplications, prayers and intercessions and giving of thanks be made for all men, for kings and all who are in authority, that we may lead a quiet and peaceable life in all goodness and reverence. For this is good and acceptable in the sight of God our Savior, who desires all men to be saved and to come to the knowledge of the truth" (1 Timothy 2:1-4).

Those who lead nations are so important to God, that He places them in first priority in the prayers of the believer. A righteous president lifts up and dignifies the country, while a corrupt president brings the whole nation to ruin. Solomon said that when the highest ruler is unjust, all those who govern under him are unjust, but when he is just, all those under him are just. Justice builds up a nation, but sin makes the people ashamed.

The Lord said: "Ask of me and I will give you the nations for your inheritance, and the ends of the earth for your possession" (Psalm 2:8). When a believer feels called by God to be a part of the future of his country, it is important that:

- His life is consecrated completely to God, always giving a good testimony.
- He knows he is called by God to fill that role, and he is not doing it motivated by his own interests.
- He always maintains ample spiritual covering, since he will be entering territory that the enemy has wanted to control throughout the ages.
- He always realizes that he is the instrument that God is using to establish His Kingdom on earth, remembering that we should not do anything through contention or vainglory.

"Eternal Father, when I see Your wonders, Your acts and miracles; when I receive your grace and Your forgiveness, I realize how great You are. The universe is in Your hands. You are the Most High, All Powerful One and because of Your love, You despised Your own nature and took on human form to give me the redemption that my soul needed. Even though the nations are in Your hands and each of them is like a drop of water, still You had mercy and decided to adopt me as Your child. Lord, thank you because now I am in Your hands and I am the sheep of Your pasture, and nobody will snatch me from Your side. I fall on my face before You and declare that You are my King. Amen."

Epilogue

It is important that these ten prayer steps, which touch the Father's heart, become part of your life. You must practice them daily. The items covered in this topic will serve as a helpful guide so you can start today. In the measure that you exercise them in prayer, you will expand your vocabulary. The Holy Spirit will help you so that the words will flow until prayer becomes a way of life for you.